My journey to the flight deck.

First Published: 2018
Copyright © Ben Rourke

Connect on social.

@ Rourkey79

@ Rourkeyshots

@ Ben Rourke

@ Aspire Pilot

Images by:

Mark Rourke (Cover photo also)
Kevin Knights
Paul Davey
My lovely SJCam 4000hd

About me

Thank you very much for showing interest in my book, I am Ben the author of this book, and am 18 years old, at the time of publishing, living in the East of England. Ever since I was two years old I have had a huge passion for transport, in general. At an early age, this, was mostly buses and trains. I would go to Ipswich train station, with my grandad, for the day, and be content for hours, scribbling down the numbers of each train. Similarly, when going to dog shows, with my Grandparents, I looked out for special lorries and coaches, I think it was this that really spurred my passion for transport on, as I had visited more of England than most adults, before I was 8 years old. The reason I spent such a large amount of time with my grandparents, was, because I didn't have a father. From my birth, I had been brought up by my strong single mother, who has done an incredible job of shaping me into who I am today. Subsequently, my grandad and grandma helped my mum, to take care of me, whilst she worked hard to provide, for both herself, me, and my autistic brother. This brought challenges to the family, as my brother was so demanding to look after, without the presence of a male figure. Fortunately, after six years of my brother being born, a new male figure came on the scene, in the form of my step father, Shane. This brought stability to the family, but by no means wealth. Although, some extra cash flow into the family, from an extra earner, did allow one of my first holidays abroad. This is when my passion for transport took a big swerve towards aviation when I was around 12 years old. I had liked planes and enjoyed watching them, going plane-spotting with my uncle, an ex-mechanic in the Royal Navy (800 Naval Air Squadron). But at 12 years old, as I matured, I began to see the beauty of flight, and the responsibility that pilots have. I loved it. In particular, this occurred on a First-Choice flight to Majorca. The airport ambience, the other excited passengers and the aircrafts moving around the apron combined, to immerse me, into a newly discovered world. Following this holiday, every day, I would play flight simulator and research various aspects of flight, from instrument landing systems to types of drag. From there, I had no doubt about it, I was to become a pilot! Everyone knew that too. I was researching day and night, how to make it to the right-hand seat of a jet. I then discovered the stringent medical requirements, heaps of money involved and various routes that you can go down. At the time, I started to demotivate myself. I compared myself to others, and felt that I couldn't become a pilot, because of my parent's financial situation. I lived in a council house. I couldn't get a loan for training. My parents couldn't lend me the money. But, my upbringing carried me to success. I stayed strong. I did all I could to make my dream a reality, and this book follows the reasons for my passion, my success and my mistakes. It gives an insight into the journey of a potentially disadvantaged teenager, and the struggles one may face. But for me, most importantly, the book is to share the wonder of flight and to inspire young people, to achieve their dreams. This is the first book in the series, hopefully, leading up to me becoming an airline pilot and leads up to the biggest days of a pilot's life, the first solo, and acquiring a private pilot's licence.

My childhood was fairly unusual, although most things that were unusual, lead me to love the world of aviation.

Contents

Section 1. Why do I want to become a pilot?

From one extreme to the other	1
Forgotten senses	11
Lunch with the birds	16
Our favourite machines	20
Sharing the passion	24

Section 2. My flying diary

Taking baby steps	30
The leap of faith	39
Could I make it this time?	51
The summer of my life	61

Section 3. Misc

My top 5 tips to aspiring aviators	92
To those that helped me	94

This book came into being because of my huge love of aviation. There wasn't too much written by people my age, so I thought that I could write a book to try and inspire people to follow their dreams, as well as to provide advice from my experiences. When asked why I love the world of aviation, it's incredibly hard for me to produce a straight answer; instead my mind goes on a journey, and in the first half of the book, you can follow just what thoughts go through my mind when I am asked 'Ben why do you want to be a pilot?'

From one extreme to the other.

It's 3 am, the ever-aggravating Samsung S6 Alarm makes me curse under my breath, however this time, instead of rolling over, slipping into light sleep like a lazy teenager, I hastily leap out of bed, or at least in contrast to the normal struggle. Like a stage light, the lamp illuminates the palace like room, shining off the varnished wooden floor. Those powerful, hot showers in the 5 star hotels warm my body, lighting my wick, and after getting dressed, slurping on a lovely hot tea, me and my Mum quietly make our way, to the reception. It's vacant, except for one other man, and with a cheery farewell my Mum and I slide into the taxi, for the short drive to Madrid's airport. After a short while whizzing around the roads filled with the orange haze of streetlights omnipresent in busy cities, we reach the main road leading to the terminal. There, in the distance, the terminal is asleep, resting, waiting to be awakened by the plague of travellers scooting across its shiny, polished floor, catching flights, stretching around the globe. The airport is the confluence, of streams of people, emerging from the surrounding sprawling metropolis. Approaching the sliding doors, the terminal, a microcosm lays behind, bringing out the best of times. First holidays, honeymoons, successful business trips and pilot's careers all originate in this seemingly idyllic location. However, the environment that lay behind those sliding doors may contain forlorn figures, grown bored by the blasé comings and goings. This is rare however, with aviation so very safe and exciting at the same time, with the airport usually filled with a joyous vibe. As we step through the doors, we leave the hot and cold, smells of cigarettes and fumes, humdrum of vehicle engines and jet engines. We enter another climate. It's fresh, at perfect temperature. Cleanliness replaces the cigarettes and fumes, chimes and chatter in place of rumbling Rolls Royce's. An obstacle course lays ahead. First the dreaded security. Speed is everything here, "remove iPads, cameras, and phones," the rush sends people panicking, shaking as they attempt to fit everything into the ever-shrinking trays. Next, security doesn't even have to ask, before I present myself to them, to be searched, in which I envisaged the blaring bleep that never leaves me alone, whenever I step through. I make it to the maze of duty free. Surrounding me, are shelves of overpriced products, I could buy elsewhere for half the price. But the bright lights, glamorous sales assistants and cheery music make passing through, part of the 'airport experience' I crave. I do prefer the next part of our course, food! Like a food hall. Restaurants, cafes, kiosks offer anything from gourmet burgers to ice creams, caviar to chips. Never passing this section, without stopping, this time at McDonalds, we continue to the end of our obstacle course, the gate. Still very early, out the window it is pitch black, sprinkled with a handful of red and white lights. The planes, which will later come to life, with rivers of thrust trailing behind then, punching a hole through the fluffy white clouds, sit seemingly dormant. The hive of activity, normally present around them, is vacant. The rushing passengers are absent too. We take a seat, watching the watch hand spin around its axis. In a sudden fashion, like a tidal surge, scores of passengers fill the gate area. It becomes a hive of activity. The dark cockpits, become illuminated, occupied by cheery captains, the darkness outside turns to a red, orange, yellow, perfect sunrise. The baggage vehicles begin whizzing around, the airport has awakened. Coming from the hinterlands of the east, I love the buzz of activity, immersed in the movement of many. Opposite to many though, I don't seek tranquillity, but instead, love the rush of people, loving the locations where people collect for which they are on never ending journeys, in their busy lives. Isolation brings a barrier for me, where I feel distant and unconnected to the global to and fro. A queue forms ahead, for which like children, people seem to be obsessed by getting on the plane as quickly as possible. Once they have satisfied themselves, by reaching their pre-assigned seats, minutes before us, we make our way down the final physical connection, between the plane and the outside world, other than the ground itself, the air bridge. Ahead, an open door, and a cheery flight attendant, welcome us into the aluminium capsule, which will take us thirty six thousand feet away from Earth. The British Airways Cityflyer Embraer E170 has just 2 seats each side, and an abundance of legroom, so I soon make myself comfortable without much effort. Despite being 6.30 AM, the temperature in Madrid is still mid-twenties, and so the whirling blow of air is released from the overhead nozzle, which so many become fond of fiddling with, throughout the flight. The captain then welcomes us aboard her aircraft. Natalie, lets us know in her mellow voice, that the flight is to be smooth, and that for once the weather is very nice in London. She lets us know, that as well as providing great service, the cabin crew are responsible for our safety. It's a sense of professionalism, that pilots and cabin crew demonstrate, in order for the lives, which they take into their control, to arrive safe and well, similar to Train Drivers and Bus Drivers, but with different capacity and complexity. Each member of crew must remain vigilant with procedures, giving an efficient, safe flow, to the whole flight process. We soon get pushed back, edging further, from norm. As we bump along the long taxiway, planes can be seen taking off and landing, disconnecting and reconnecting, with earth. Passengers are excited, to see the movements across the airfield, and spend time marvelling the scenes in which, they themselves, will be experiencing in a short time. Like on a roller coaster, the anticipation of experiencing new dimensions, is exciting for many. The intense acceleration, is felt, as we begin our takeoff roll. The streams of thrust flow behind us, whilst the lumps and bumps, add perspective, to the increasing speed. As the bumps grow louder, and movements more twitchy, the wheels pay their final farewell to earth, before they emerge once more, over a city of stark contrast. Pushed lightly into our seats by the new vertical dimension, we edge further and further from norm, as the Madrid suburbs race past the windows. The cars become toy like and streams like a pencil line. More emerges into view, changing the perspective in the way we see our planet. The 1 hour journey across Madrid, becomes a few centimetres. The Winding Ebro River, a few miles. The high peaks of the Pyrenees, standing thousands of feet high, few inches higher than the land bordering them. For any journey, an aircraft will fly over places of stark contrast. For part of the journey, I look down at the bronzed Iberian countryside. My mind, dissolves into imagination, as I catch a glimpse of tiny Spanish hamlets scattered around the rugged terrain, in the expanse, of the desolate, interior landscape. There I see, in my imagination, the mothers making their way to collect bread from the local bakery, the children scuttling across the dusty, rocky tracks to their small, village school, whilst their fathers, round up their cattle, to provide for their families. It makes me pause for a moment. The closest place, on the surface we live on, to us, is a place, where we would struggle, without Internet and proper electricity. It adds the sense that globalisation, is funnelled into an aircraft at the start of its journey, and is encapsulated, as it makes its voyage across the boundless skies. As the wings cut through the cold high air, the places passing underneath, contain people, who will never be able to experience such a thing, and may not even leave their country or region. Closing down on London, we pass over the Bay of Biscay and the Channel, where like tiny tablets, long vessels, sail across the high seas. Boats always fascinate me, maybe being, because their existence, on the open oceans, are most similar to the unique event of flying. The complex air, in which planes fly in, replicate the surging currents of water. Similar to Tundra for land, the high atmosphere sky and vast open seas are barren, rarely visited by normal, everyday life. The flying machines, themselves, are equalled by similarly exquisite manufacturing. When flying over water, rather than being disconcerting, it brings out the relationship between the skies and seas, making a rather more 'homely' feeling. All these places, and views, seem to be a big factor in the relationship between aviation, and the young, that are amazed by it. Whether it be the cyan coastline of Cayo Coco, or the soaring skyscrapers of Shanghai, heads turn to the plastic inside windows in awe, at our planet, seen in a new perspective. Our Cityflyer flight, is drawing to a close. Despite an inversion layer in the atmosphere, trapping the city of London's fumes and dust, causing reduced visibility, the unmistakable twisting Thames shaping the Capitals layout, the gherkin standing tall in its gentrified grounds, the O2 looking like an utter monstrosity of a building, can all be clearly viewed from above. Whether it be, the alpine mountains in Geneva or Turin, the gorgeous beaches of Corfu or Tenerife, the complex cityscapes of Paris or Athens or the barren grounds of Sharm El Sheikh or Monastir, the Final approach brings clarity, to the things we witness, as we near normality. Almost Godlike, we look down on the flow of life below, the trains on their pre laid tracks, the cars on their set roads, the pedestrians on following footpaths. As the wheels are dropped, over the new city, we begin to slow. For a brief moment, I begin to get slightly apprehensive and nervous. Not about the landing itself, but instead the events proceeding it. Flight offers salvation from the problems on the ground. The queues, the people who cause problems, the infinite delays from traffic and lateness. More so for a longer flight, disembarking feels like emerging, slightly into the unknown, leaving the comfort of peace, safety and care, for the standard rhythm of life on the ground that never slows.

Soon enough, we navigate through the shoals of complacent business men in the sea of passengers flowing through London City Airport, and take the DLR to Liverpool Street, from where we take the intercity service, back home. Here I realise the magic which preceded my journey home. All unfolded from the glamorous hotel room, where I was awakened, by my pesky alarm. From then, I entered the unique world of aviation, passing over high seas and Spanish hamlets, looking down on earth. Over London, the views were breath-taking. However, all of this is replaced, by a far simpler, yet more powerful feeling. Four hours before, I was in Spain's Capital, 800 miles away, and now I'm eating Lunch, on an English train, a feeling that never gets old and certainly never will.

The afternoon sun was high, the skies were blue, but it was colder, with a faint breeze homing in off the North Sea. I was syncing back into English life, after days in Spain, dealing with a phenomenon known as Place Lag, something beautifully described, and explored, by the writer and pilot Mark Vanhoenacker, in his wonderful book, Skyfaring. On this day, I was truly spreading my wings, indulging in all extremes, of flying itself; I was to go from passenger to pilot, spectator to controller. I arrived at my local airfield, Beccles, for an impromptu flying lesson, courtesy of my keen instructor, Stuart. The mixture of smells, of freshly mown grass, controllers munching on jam sandwiches, sat outside soaking up some rays, the occasional purr of a classic Cessna in the circuit, set the perfect summertime scene. Almost metaphoric, the fence surrounding the airport represents the opportunity, and progress, I have made. My Juvenile self, would gaze at the pilots getting in to their pride and joys, starting their chugging engines, leaping into the boundless skies, breaking its bonds, the fence was the blockade, between me, and my dreams. Now on this day, I open the gate, and slowly walk across the perfectly green, freshly cut grass. I have already achieved a childhood dream, stepping the other side, of the restrictive fence. I check the aircraft, with a feeling of care and responsibility, making sure every aspect, is up to standards. I bid farewell to those on the ground, once more, before myself and Stuart struggle into, the cramped, 1960's Cessna 150. Even though I had done this nearly 8 times before, the inner satisfaction of replicating those I once admired, and still do, never leaves me. The heart of the engine starts to beat. The soul of the plane, myself and Stuart, make a radio call to the guardian of the skies, the controllers. Releasing the brakes, and rolling across the ground, we have the intention of flight, so in terms of aviation law, the flight has begun. In front of me, lays a third of runway, preserved for use, from World War 2. Around 70 years ago, in front of my very eyes, I would witness the fighters, such as the De Havilland Mosquito, rumbling down the tarmac, roaring up into the blackening clouds, destroying the Germans, serving our country. Our heroes, once raced down this runway, and now it's my turn! Now plagued with potholes and cracks, we bump along, backtracking, before pivoting around, aligning with the quarter mile, of concrete. Here, for a matter of seconds, one of the greatest powers of flight exists, the fact, that if it was road, it would take us a quarter of mile, but because it's runway, it can take us anywhere. As our tiny Cessna lurches forwards, the rapid gyration of the propeller generates a faint black haze ahead. The noise cancelling headphones, blank any whisper of engine noise, leaking into my ears, as we twitch left and right, speeding down the runway. Within seconds, for the second time in the day, the wheels disconnect with earth, as we accelerate into freedom. On a hot summer day akin to this, vast vertical movements of air known as thermals, make the air choppy, and bumpy. If the air, was made visible, large whirlwinds, would be seen, spiralling and tumbling, like ripping ocean currents. In a direct sense, my soft, weak hands movements on the tiny worn black metal yoke, are amplified. With the twist of my wrist, I can roll and loop, dive toward the ground or climb high, above the clouds, into a different day. The haze, diminishing views over London earlier, are present over Suffolk too. We speak to Radar control at Norwich; a lady with a soft, soothing, reassuring voice tells us she has us, on her radar. Under her watchful eyes, I apply full power, raising the nose, to ascend above the milky murk. I see, just a few miles ahead, when my beady eyes swing around their sockets, looking out for other aviators. Five thousand feet, above Earth, we emerge from the low-level scum, into perfectly clear, silky smooth air. Such experiences, draws the separation that flight brings, piercing into new heights, into the bright, different days. More so, on days, where cloud hangs, oppressive over earth. Days on earth, where rain, batters its surface. Days where light, is absent, for the entire day. Breaking through the overcast skies, we are made to realise, it's the weather which dictates the day, deciding the fate of any plans. On a misty, January morning, it may be, that just one hundred feet above Earth, a completely different day exists. I encounter, the same joys of flight, experienced earlier, on the memorable August day. The stunning coastline below, glimmers in the golden, afternoon sun, masked by a grim haze. Cars become toy like, rivers and roads, like pencil lines. However, the views and observations are accompanied by a sense of fulfilment, as I guide the flying machine, through the still skies of Suffolk. Being in control of a car for the first time was unreal, taking the wheel of a vehicle, of great power, into the palms, of my nervous hands. But I drove along the roads, obeying rule after rule, cautious of the crazy citizens, springing out from everywhere. When I first took a plane into my hands, some years ago, the amount of freedom hit me. I could wander the skies, like a lost soul hunting for an oasis, across a vast desert. Upwards was open to explore too. Few years later, I was in the position I was in now. I could push the black throttle lever forwards, pulling back on the yoke. I could enter new heights by myself. Entering skies which grew cold, and breathing made harder, by the thin air. Stuart, sat beside me, had noticed too, what I had mentioned to him. The oil pressure of the engine was dropping, the temperature rising. In the air, there are no lay-bys. The closest equivalent being a return to the airfield, or a forced landing into a farmer's field. With the airfield almost below us, Stuart took control and in a calm, swift manor, he cut the throttle and dived us into the murk beneath. Popping back into the clear, we end up on a very high final approach, gliding back to safety. Luckily, the problem wasn't serious, with the cause being a thick type of oil. Through intuition, pilots become alert, dealing with problems quickly, and calmly. As aviators, we aspire to be senior captains, with the ultimate responsibility of flight. A common saying, an ex RAF pilot reminded me of, at breakfast, is 'pilots can become bold, they can also grow old. But they never become old and bold'.

I thank Stuart, and fill in paperwork, as we drive home. I feel a sense of accomplishment as my hour column builds, edging closer to my aspirations of flying others, becoming more alert, and assessing risk. The similarities and contrasts on this day, make me realise why, as aspiring aviators, we want to be pilots. It's what I call, 'the pilot earth'. The crust and mantle represents the feelings we get from the atmosphere and views, people and motion. But the inner core. The burning desire. Is command. The command of flight.

High above the suburbs of Madrid at sunset.

The controls that give me the command of flight.
Cessna 150 G-AWTX.

Forgotten Senses

thought

It's a bitterly cold January morning. Next to my uncle, I stand on the frosty grass of Myrtle Avenue, Heathrow's famous plane spotting location. Surrounding me, hordes of similar people, aiming their cameras like snipers, hunting down elusive airliners, are scattered around the grassy patch. Once a minute, for the entire day, the sounds of car engines, conversation, trains and nearby horses are silenced by the bassy drone, of turbine engines from the planes, which pass hundreds of feet above. Wide bodies such as the A380, 747 and A350s pass. Smaller types such as the A320, 737 and 757s fill the gaps. After a while, I notice the smaller aluminium tubes, dwarfed by the colossal queens of the skies, become less of a spectacle. Instead, the camera shutters are only fired at the biggest aircrafts. I begin to wonder why this is. Why do we like planes in the first place? It must be a huge passion, because our feet are like ice blocks to witness them! Like most things in aviation, I believe the obsession with the flying machines themselves links to the unique nature, of what the whole world of flight entails. Buses, coaches, lorries all drive along a road held up by it. Boats skim on the surface of water, floating on the fluid substance. Trains stick to the tracks like magnets. But when we think of flying, unless we have studied it, it is almost magic. How can it be, that a one hundred tonne mass, can be held aloft by the air itself? It fascinates so many, even those, whose hobby is not aircraft. Whenever I backtrack the runway at my home airport, I often see young families, at the end, watching the buzzing planes launch into the blue skies. For young children, it is both strange and unique, to see an engine powered vehicle, leave the normality of ground, for the skies, they may rarely look. Recently, I had the opportunity to visit the hangars, of Lufthansa Technik, in Frankfurt. The monstrous hangars, overlook the airport, spanning hundreds of acres. When I entered the glass doors, the view hit me. It was simply jaw dropping. The hangar is dark from the colossal jets casting their shadows on the concrete ground. I'm with my uncle and his friend, a fellow avgeek. Our hosts are employees and past employees. When approaching the A380, I get a strange sense of excitement. The sense that I am entering something rarely accessible from this perspective, something which belongs away from the closure of the hangar, and instead, in the freedom of the skies. Rather than entering through a jetway, we struggle up the metal stairs, only normally found at remote airports. Here, the wings can be seen sweeping back, with the engines hanging below. As the pilot advances the throttles, these fans would spin around like a whirlwind, with a ground shaking rumble. As Jeremy Clarkson commonly says. "POWER!" These engines take the plane away from us, on the ground, to great heights. Just today, as I write this, I witnessed something physically metaphoric of what flight entails. As a Luxair Dash 8 departed the ground, within seconds, it was quite literally swallowed up by the oppressive cloud lingering over London, into its new world. I, on the pavement, felt, now disconnected from the aircraft, absent from its journey. A feeling reflective of those on board. Sights are just tiny snippets, just moments.

I am often guilty of eavesdropping conversations on board. Where people become friends for the hours of the flight, they discuss the reasons for travel, some as small as for leisure, some as big as weddings or competing in the Olympics. So, on the A380 I walked the length of in the Frankfurt hangar, over 500 unheard stories existed with each rotation, as the jet disappeared, into the clouds above.

Sound

When scooting around the streets of London or striding through Hyde Park, every minute, the sound of disrupted air and spinning fan blades, cuts through the mumble of everyday sounds. People look skyward, knowing the sound instinctively. Often, the presence of planes many thousands of feet above us, is only revealed by the rumbling sound they produce, with us looking up hopelessly into the glare. Noise has become one of the major issues of flight, but for us aviation lovers, it's just another quality of it. Power can be translated through sound. At air shows, the piercing sound of the glowing afterburners catches people by surprise, causing them to cover their ears, and the sound almost becomes a feeling as it vibrates our bodies. Some lucky souls, have witnessed a sonic boom, produced from the sheer speed of fast jets, which almost breaks physics, causing an explosion of sound. When we fly on older aircraft, the sound is more exciting, more powerful, more capturing. When sitting in front of the engine, we hear a phenomenon called Buzzsaw. Where like an American muscle beast, the jet engines produce an unmistakable buzzing roar, as each fan blade tip passes the speed of sound. The louder the better for us! Those familiar with the procedures during flight can associate sounds with each stage of flight. When we get pushed from the gate, the eerie hush that fills the cabin as the whirling air conditioning sound is diminished, signifies the engines are about to start. The repetitive, hydraulic sound, on Airbuses, like a barking dog, signals the transfer of hydraulic fluid usually when just one engine is operating. The electrical whine, during flight, indicates the movement of flaps, usually for take-off and landing. The nearing conclusion of the flight is often sensed coming from the loud rushing sound of air as the gear is lowered. Despite this link of sound to power and procedure, some aviators are fond of the silence and tranquillity that some forms of flight offer. Without an engine, gliders soar through the air, lifted by hot rising air. No sounds of air traffic control, no purring engine, just the gentle rush of air swooping over the glider. But, however quiet the sound gliders produce, pilots still use sound for their own safety. Approaching a stall, the gentle rush of air becomes absent, and absolute silence becomes more of a fright than pleasure. Sound maybe not be perceived to be significant to flight and we don't often associate it with the wonder of flight, but without it, the sense power and propulsion would be reduced, to a rather docile, physical quality, with a lack of immersion.

Smell

It's a sunny, calm summer afternoon at Beccles airfield. I stand on a slightly damp, slippery, silver ladder, dipping the tanks of the Cessna 150, to check the fuel. There in front of me, the King of the airfield, the majestic Cessna Caravan sits resting, as parachutists, pumped full of adrenaline, pile into the back of its modified cabin. Ready to go, the turbine engine sparks into life, the propeller spins faster and faster. Standing behind, in its wake, I get unsettled by the gusts of air as the propeller spins faster and faster. Immediately, my nose catches the scent of Jet A1 fuel. The smell of kerosene, if I was deaf and blind, could reveal the presence of the aircraft. Often in aviation crashes, victims describe the smell of kerosene, an unmistakable scent that lingers in the air, often smelt around busy airfields. I think to myself, what if I could not smell aviation? It would just become a world of sound and sight. We seemingly take smells and sound for granted. When people express their feelings about aviation, it's in terms of views and motion, time and place. But when we think of it, without the sounds and smell, aviation would become increasingly dull, and as aviators and avgeeks, we seek the little things that makes flight so special. As a person drawn to flight, you will see the expressions used to describe sound and smell, but if written by a traveller instead, the book would be just a concoction of views and feelings, without the precise particularities, of the things we seek, in the world of flight.

Sight, sound and smell.

Lunch with the birds

It's a stunning clear, sunny, August morning in Suffolk. The vibrant green grass of the fields are soaked with morning dew and a light breeze makes the brown branches bob up and down. My mum drives along the lazy Sunday roads. Only families or couples populate these quiet roads. Later on, in their grandma's dining rooms, the families that we pass, will maybe enjoy roast dinners and jam roly poly. My Mum too will enjoy lunch with my Dad and Sister at the local restaurant. But what about me? I won't be on earth to have lunch. I will be high above it, enjoying lunch in the sky. Arriving at the gliding club, there is always a sense of teamwork. As we wheel out the purest flying machines, that's gliders, another small group are busy preparing the bus, which is the control room for the day. Or more precisely, home of the cuppa teas! The gentle, warm breeze makes me feel relaxed and calm in my T-shirt, as I walk the gliders to the end of the runway. The haste you would expect is non-existent. Instead, a chilled, slow vibe fills the air. For good reason, too, as we await the power of our flight to arrive. Like tiny balls of cotton wool, small wisps of perfectly white cloud grow into shadow casting giants. Although invisible, a violent, strong circulation of air exists. Like a jet wash fired upwards, the air is propelled sky bound to its destiny, where it condenses, and is turned to cloud. Signalling this invisible atmospheric wonder, the cute, fluffy white clouds bring good news, making the older members of the club seem a lot younger. After launching some excited pilots sky bound, my time finally arrives, to depart normality, and enjoy one of the purest forms of flight there is. I strap on my parachute, regardless of the irony in putting on such a thing with the intention of flight, and leave the bus for the glider, resting on the hot black tarmac. Checked and ready, I pull down the canopy, shutting out all the doubts and problems, and dissolve into a world of determination and aspiration. The metal winch cable tightens; motion kicks in. With a sudden jerk, the cable bolts towards its origin, taking us with it. Within seconds, the wings gain lift, taking us skyward. The g force pushes me tightly into my cramped seat, as we climb like a rocket. Nearing one thousand feet, the acceleration reduces, and with a loud BANG, the winch cable back releases. Now two steps closer to heaven, my instructor and I grace the skies above the local villages, where the people look up to see a pure white silent flying machine gracefully twist and turn. We do what's known colloquially in the gliding world as 'Scratching' around for thermals, where we turn left and right under the fluffy white clouds. Although the main reason to do such a thing, is to take us higher, making our flight longer, I do get the sense from my fellow pilots, thermaling, is far more than that. Thermaling becomes a challenge. To rise up on the warm air is a unique experience. The satisfaction of it however, drives a student glider pilot to go solo and embark on his or her own unforgettable journeys. No matter how long glider pilots have been flying, the thermal always seems to make them excited, expressed by a slight chuckle or maybe words of accomplishment. Dave (my instructor) and I do just that. We fly slowly towards a large darkening cloud. As we approach, like driving on a road with many potholes, we get the occasional shudder as the falling air of the convection currents strike our wings, pushing us down. Then suddenly, like speeding over a humped bridge, the unforgettable high pitched beeping variometer sounds excited, with the positive G making me feel light. We quickly glance left, it's clear, so we turn whilst the excited sounding vario continues to beep away. Like a lost car around a roundabout, we circle round and round as we continue to go up and up. Each minute, the ground grows further and further. Approaching 3000ft the coast comes to view. Getting higher, the air reaches its end, where it condenses to cloud. We are now left to glide through the still summer air. In the straight glide the speed reduces to fifty and the rush of air grows quiet. Peace fills the air, as I admire the local area, uninterrupted by the drone of an engine. Like an Albatross, the glider I'm flying, floats on the air, occasionally making a gentle turn, without a beat of a wing. We encounter several of these moments of serenity, but one stood out to me that day. Penetrating into the plume of air ahead, we circled round and round once more. But, as we looked by our wing, seagulls and Buzzards joined the roundabout of air, and with each one hundred feet we gained, the majestic birds would also glide up with us. I looked down to see a small town, Stowmarket. Here at this hour, Sunday lunches would be served. But rather than being glued to the normality of earth to enjoy it, I wrestled free to embrace our wildlife and mimic their actions to stay aloft. So instead, I ate my tuna sandwiches with the birds! Colliding with earth, I didn't feel upset that I was no longer airborne, instead refreshed and accomplished. When driving home, my brain was set on repeat of the glorious scenes, as I ate lunch with the birds!

A beautiful quote by Neil Armstrong describes the beauty of gliding. 'Gliders, sail planes, they're wonderful flying machines. It's the closest you can come to being a bird' and on that afternoon I felt just that, just like a bird. I began to glide when I was 15. I wanted to begin flying and satisfy my desires of flight in a way where my bank account would remain existent. I searched my local gliding club and booked a trial lesson. Arriving at the airfield, my face lit up to see a flying machine at arm's reach. Having that cliché teenager impression that if I can fly the biggest airliner on flight simulator then I can easily fly anything, I stepped into the glider. My hand sat resting on the control stick as we were towed skyward by the tug, and we stayed exactly behind it, like intercepting it as a fighter jet. Once at 3000ft my instructor pulled the cable and we turned left. Settling the aircraft into steady straight flight, controls were handed to me to have my first go at flying a glider. I kept it level, but when turning, it soon developed into a descending, sliding mess. The experience highlighted to me, that to learn to fly, I had a way to go. With each launch I felt more confident and ultimately in control. Every single flight I had learnt something new, whether that was smaller things such as turning correctly and trimming correctly or bigger things such as my first takeoff and landing. This, in itself, is the beauty of gliding, and in fact any flying activity. You never, ever stop learning. And the abilities to develop new skills or master old ones are endless!

'Like an Albatross' gliding at Rattlesden gliding club 2015.

The view from the quietest cockpit going.

19

Our Favourite Machines

Tied to the ground ahead, the tiny Cessna 150 awaits its next set of aviators on the average partly cloudy, summer Saturday. Already passing the boundary of my dreams, the flying machines I spent so long marvelling, now sit just an arm reach away. The propeller sits still at the front, with long aero foil shaped wings stretching out wide, the tailplane at the rear stands tall with the red beacon siting restful on the top. With any aircraft, the thing that makes them a plane is the wings, the things that allow flight, from the production of lift. Without these long, fairly flat pieces of aluminium, the plane would sit grounded and look no different to those vehicles permanently stuck like a magnet to earth. When we see wings, it's a signal of our unique love, flight. On the walk around I softly run my hands along the surfaces, testing and assessing their structural integrity, for the powerful forces they will experience in a short while. The plane possesses a large amount of lightness and flexibility, I can move it easily with just a single hand, something hugely unexpected. On the walk around, things appear that associate the aircraft with a vehicle more familiar with me. We check the oil, using the dip stick found on most cars. We check the shiny metallic disc brakes, found on bikes. Aerials stick out, ready to catch the airwaves. And the lights that shine brightly, similar to the cars headlights. But the event of flight seems far more substantial. Like preparing a car for a journey into the unknown, we carefully scan the exterior, interior and the liquids, for the sky in barren and desolate and the plane possesses gravitational potential energy, a dangerous possession, high up in an unlikely event. We don't even trust the fuel gauges, and use a ladder to reach over and dip the fuel tanks to ensure the tanks don't run dry, leaving us to glide.

Once upon a time at Stansted airport on a freezing cold winters days, I got an unexpected call. A Titan Airways Captain who I came to know, invited me to the company's hangar at the airport. With that, my grandad and I departed the slippery muddy slope we stood on, to view the aircraft hundreds of meters away and headed to the hangar. Arriving at Titans hangar, we met up with Richard, who looked very smart and was enthusiastic about showing us around. Signing the entry sheet, we placed our lanyards on (all very official) and opened the door into the large hangar. Before the sight of a Boeing 757 even crossed my mind, the freezing air in the hanger made it more like stepping into a large freezer than a hangar and sent me into a shivering trance! Soon accustomed to the artic temperature, the large flying machine sitting dormant, enclosed in the building, struck me. Unlike the smaller aircraft, where the wings add fascination to the machine, the large Rolls Royce RB211 engines took centre stage. Just moments ago, I stood observing these powerful aircraft launch into the Essex skies, carrying skiers to the slopes of Salzburg, and now I'm sat inside one's engine. The large fan blades that spin round, chopping through the air, sit still. It always strikes me how a single lever, can control these beasts, which can produce over forty thousand pounds of thrust. That's two thirds the weight of the aircraft available in thrust! The whole aircraft looks incredible as the hanger dwarfs it. A small business jet sits beside it, adding perspective. Whenever I fly, I always ask the cheerful cabin crew if I can visit the pilots in the flight deck, no matter how many times I've been in that particular types cockpit. The cockpit possesses a different kind of journey. Enclosed, a hive of activity from start to finish takes place. Just 2 people interact, sharing the jobs. Each time I enter, the displays and buttons, that are more meaningful to me, make me excited. Often, I am invited to take a seat and when seated, the pilots always seem impressed by my knowledge of the plane. However, this is through passion and constant interaction with aviation. The flight simulator is good, but it lacks any atmosphere. Once in the cockpit, you can feel the aircraft breathing, you can feel the hydraulics flow like blood in arteries, it feels alive. The cockpit is often described as the best office in the world. The views are great and the seats are incredibly comfortable. But it's the operation of the machine that makes this place so special. Turning on the seatbelt sign made my day in the hangar, with a ding and a brief sentence "cabin crew ten minutes to landing!"

The outside of the aircraft is incredible. We see the mechanisms that allows flight to commence. Although it's nice to stand back and watch flight, it's normal for us to want to break the boundaries and get closer. There are many reasons why people like flying machines. If I was to be asked the question, I would answer by saying, I love planes for what they allow us to do. They represent freedom and they add new dimension to earth. Planes are unique. Trains move in two directions on a single axis, cars, ships, bikes have two, but planes, they have three. But others may respond differently, there's many variables that accumulate to drag someone to the love of flight. Often however, the love comes from nowhere, with no family background in aviation, people just grow to love it. I have always loved transport, copying down bus timetables, writing down the Lorries and busses we pass, keeping a travel diary. I believe my love of aviation was born from this. On my first flight as a growing boy to Majorca I realised the magic of flight, standing stuck to the terminal window like glue. Peeled away, I entered the plane, it was just like a glorified bus! Carrying similar numbers of passengers, an aircraft is just a flying bus, with many wonders added to the fairly dull experience of riding a bus. And with that, I was truly hooked.

Aesthetics play a huge part in our love of planes. The queen of the skies, the Boeing 747, even turns the heads of people not even remotely interested in flight. The hump at the front of the fuselage, the four huge engines mounted on the sweeping wings. It's just come to be labelled the Jumbo Jet, and everyone knows that. I believe that in a contradictory sense that nature and aviation are similar to one another. The program 'Planet Earth' by Sir David Attenborough, attracts millions of viewers amazed by the magical scenes of Mother Nature. Many who watch it though, have little interest in nature. If they are on holiday somewhere like Africa, where there's lots of nature, then maybe they will become interested, but it isn't their everyday hobby. Planes are the same, whenever people venture on their travels, they are always amazed by the planes whizzing around the airport and sky, talking to one another about the machines they see. The biggest always seem to grab more attention. People look at the A380 and 747 with more wonder and amazement, it's almost like 'aircraft discrimination', where relative to the surroundings the biggest, most complex aircraft take centre stage, just like the Cessna Caravan is the king of the small Suffolk airfield, Beccles. I believe people come to love aviation due to its unique nature. The machines are complex, with mechanisms that you could barely consider to be possible, with miles of electronics and a maze of hydraulic lines, perfectly linked up to form a working aircraft. Looking high up into the blue sky, we dream of beautiful places, having a blast of a time. Planes allow theses dreams to live and make the seemingly impossible, entirely possible.

Cessna 'India Gulf' at Beccles Airfield on a hot summer evening.

Sharing the Passion

It's a glorious summer morning, I'm stood with my grandad, firing our shutters, hunting down elusive airliners on top of the infamous muddy mound at Stansted airport. After a while, between the gaps, we take a bite from our picnic. However, each time we do this something interesting happens, of course! As the sun arced around, getting higher in the sky, the morning dew was burnt off leaving a fine dry day. Around an hour later, I and my grandad were growing increasingly bored by the repetition of the movements at the location. In the trees lining the fence, a lone figure emerged walking in our direction. With a camera in one hand, it was obvious he was here to capture the fine machines arriving and departing. Arriving at the mound, a quick customary hello was exchanged before silence filled the air as the shutters clicked away. My Grandad remarked "I wonder where those lucky buggers are off to." Like a little tiny catalyst for a massive explosion, a simple response from the boy, on top of the mound, created a lifetime friendship. To my Grandad's enquiry, the boy responded "Lanzarote." I begin to talk to him, after the display of knowledge, for a potential conversation about our similar love. Proceeding this, the rest of the day was fantastic and we added one another on social media, talk regularly and even go on trips across Europe with each other.

This experience made me think, sharing the experience of aviation is exciting. It allows us to express our feelings by reliving precious moments as we tell them. Often, talking to the older generation is really interesting. The experiences they have had are vibrantly told, with passion, and with clarity, as if it happened the day before. One such story was highly exhilarating, told by an ex turboprop pilot from my gliding club and goes something like this: It's a hellish winter day in London, battered by tornado like gusts, flooded by lashing rain and lit up by electric blue lightning. Just about at limits to fly, planes struggle in as they rock side to side, porpoising up and down in the air. Many flights are cancelled with so many diverting and circling. The particular flight for the pilot was from London to Amsterdam in a small turboprop. Departing safely into the grip of the dark skies, the aircraft is chucked around the sky, whilst the lightning lights up the cabin in the dismal grey clouds. Penetrating into the calm, the cruise is smooth as the world below continues to be tormented by the raging winter storm. At the time of descent, the pilot describes how icing began to show. Diving back into the ocean of cloud, the windscreen frosts up and the wings covered by a rough skin of ice. By pressing a small metal switch on the overhead panel, a rubber boot slides across the leading edge of the wing, making the wings smooth once more. Emerging into the unknown, the plane is at 45 degrees to the runway, as a stiff wind howls perpendicular to the runway. Crabbing in, the pilot describes how with a kick of the rudder, and with a hard jolt, the plane reconnects with earth, escaping the grip of the angry skies. Such a story highlights the exciting encounters which pilot's experience, displaying skill through confidence and professionalism. Being told such stories motivates me, making my passion stronger, excited to experience such moments. The older generation pass on their experience to us through intuition, and remains a reminder as to why being a pilot is such a lucrative career. In essence sharing our passion with the old motivates whilst it educates. Flying lessons are really exciting for myself, who works and learns for six days a week. On the single day off I get, flying gives me a chance to escape the mundane realities of life and indulge in something for myself which I enjoy. Getting later in the year, the roads are lit up by the golden autumn sun, whilst the orangey, red leaves litter it. Arriving at the airfield, it, too, looks equally as attractive in the new season. Excited, I enter the small, cabin like clubhouse. However, the normal greetings are more brusque than normal. I was quickly ushered outside, staggering around confused. It wasn't until I stepped round the corner onto the manoeuvring area till I realised what was happening. There, in front of me, sat a Piper PA46 Malibu, a powerful turboprop in a gleaming gold and blue paint scheme. I was being invited, with the other airfield members, to have a look around the fine machine. Sitting still on the concrete taxiway, the aircraft was resting after its flight from Biggin Hill, near London. I spoke to my fellow aviators about the delicate cockpit as we stepped inside for a closer look. The glass cockpit meant it was mostly screens with a selection of switches and buttons. Emerging from the complex flight deck, I spoke with one of the owners who began to describe the beautiful aircraft. Even though we had never met, conversation began to flow easily, as it did with my friend at Stansted. Having a fantastic tour of the marvellous machine, me and one of the other members laughed and joked as we walked back to the clubhouse, discussing our sudden new life ambitions to acquire such a beauty. Almost an hour had passed and I still hadn't flown, but I wasn't bothered, deeply immersed in the club atmosphere. I then briefed for the lesson and headed out to the aircraft for a very enjoyable flight around my local area, learning how to climb and descend. Bouncing up and down along the potholed runway, we soon come to rest on the somewhat softer grass. Upon entering the clubhouse, I saw a small group of members enjoying a cold drink in the evening sunshine. I even questioned Stuart as to whether we accidentally landed at Ibiza, judging the rare sight! Signing the relevant forms and updating my logbook, I went outside to join the small coterie of aviators. I cracked open a nice lemonade and messaged my mum, asking her to collect me in one hour; I then switched into pilot mode. Sharing moments with people with the same interests is entertaining. It allows us to express our feelings and interests, feeling the passion as we say it. Pilots will often drink together and will become good friends, as do fellow builders and hairdressers. However with flying, there's a constant attraction to its wonders, which builders may not experience, and may indeed, want to forget. Flying clubs allow us to meet similar people, fitting into our social clique. Despite my excitement that day was focused on the flying, the club turned the event of a flying lesson into more of an engaging, brilliant social experience.

Me 'sharing the passion' with my friend Conor in a Monarch Airlines Airbus A321 after a daytrip to Majorca.

The Flying Diary

In the first chapters we explored how aviation, although a common everyday thing, is a unique experience, taking us away from normal life, into something most people look forward to, and cherish. We then looked at how magical a flying lesson is, both matching and contrasting the commercial experience I had the morning before. We then inspected each of the senses leading to the experience of flight; sights, smell and sound. A pure flying experience, gliding then added a new reason to adore flight without some of these senses. Finally we explored how sharing the passion of aviation turns the encounters with it into an experience, as opposed to an event. I compiled a story modelled on some of my favourite anecdotes to display each one of these aspects, adding clarity as to why I fly. However, to get these experiences and to pursue my dreams, it requires a huge amount of hard work and determination. Unfortunately, it's not easy to make flying a career due to the high competition and the cost of training. Many people wonder what it takes and don't understand the process due to its complexity. However, I like that. It poses a challenge, which involves improvisation to break the boundaries in the way of the dream. If you are truly devoted and sacrifice both time and money, then becoming a pilot shouldn't be a struggle, but instead a challenge to be cracked only by the most determined.

Taking Baby Steps

The passion for planes was always there, but a lack of maturity made it hard to properly understand what I needed to do to become an aviator. In my early teens, I spent hours surfing through the depressing pilot forums and slipped away into a mindset of disbelief. I began to consider being a train driver or an air traffic controller as the outlooks for a job looked far more likely. This mindset even made me lose my articulate personality and just become another grumpy teenager. This wasn't right at all and after a few days, with a trip to the local airport to do some spotting, a sudden change occurred. I realised that although a lot of the aviation gossip on the forum is the truth, a lot of things written, are by people that are angry about the career prospects and lack the motivation to make it happen by other means. Disregarding this brainwashing rubbish, I allocated two hours a night to revise in year 8 (yes, I know that's crazy) and began to search for positive things on the matter. This is my first piece of advice. Don't get brainwashed by forums, although some things are true, other things are written by people that lack the willingness to sacrifice money and a comfortable lifestyle to fly. Just take it with a pinch of salt! That said, I looked at some pilot profiles and looked at what they done in their youth to reach the position they managed to secure. A common pattern began to occur, where most wrote that they joined the Air Cadets. Although not too struck on the thought of being a member of the cadets, I decided that the combination of advice from current pilots and my family seemed good enough to follow.

The cadets looked great when I looked on the website. Fantastic activities included summer camps, shooting, rock climbing, night time search and rescue missions and most importantly flying! Elated to be old enough to join, my mum took me on the first possible evening. That evening I experienced the dreaded drill, football practice and the exciting events coming up shared in the briefing. It was amazing. Within a few weeks I was a full member by doing my enrolment and getting my uniform. I felt so proud in the uniform, with a sharp crease in my trousers, courtesy of my expert, at least I thought, ironing skills. Over my two years in the cadets, I had many moments which I treasure. Night time exercises were great teamwork building activities, by having a huge amount of fun, creeping around a dark forest, hunting down the other team. There were many great sporting events, including football and athletics, one in which we did exceptionally well. I feel like the one that taught me the most about society and how life has changed was the camp we went on to North Norfolk. Armed up with a huge bag, I left home for 3 days to a random location in the military ranges, I was nothing short of petrified! However, as the minibus pulled away this worrying faded away into a world of excitement, I was still apprehensive of the happenings on camp however. Arriving in the middle of a forest, we entered a clearing surrounded by barbed wire and patrolled by armed soldiers. Exiting the bus, we headed for our luxury accommodation. Enlarged pig sheds! Copying everyone else, I unpacked my sleeping bag on the rock solid gel mattress and got ready for the march to the welcome gathering, where we met everyone and learned about what we would be up to for the next few days. It all sounded great! We headed back to our pig sheds and mingled and behaved like typical lads till the day turned into a new one, not the best idea considering we had to be up at six. That was half the fun of it though. Waking up at six, we all laughed and joked, moaned and groaned, got ready and headed for the canteen. I was amazed! We even had the luxury of a cooked breakfast. It was bound to be a great day with a start like this. And sure, it was. Our first exercise was to move through an area of forest without being spotted in the quickest time. Despite my feet getting drenched, brushing through the soaking grass, we made it in good time. Next was a small team exercise, including a tower building task, puzzles, aircraft recognition and first aid situations. This was good fun, in doing so, we were building key teamwork skills too. This was a good part of the day as we had lunch. Yum! The next event was some shooting. I'm not a natural marksman and scared of guns if anything. Laying down holding a heavy rifle wasn't exactly the most exhilarating of activities. But at least I managed to hit the target at least once. It was nice to leave the camp too. Once back, we had a rest and dinner and got ready to get up nice and early again. This day was great fun because it included my favourite activities. Geocaching and archery. The geocaching was in a large area in a big forest. Two cadets even went missing for a while! Trekking through dense bracken, dusty dirt and slippery leaves, we made our way around and didn't do well. At least we didn't get lost. We had lunch and went straight to archery which was great fun and managed to get most shots on the board, the glorious

North Norfolk sunshine helped the day become my favourite day and the people I shared the day with, were excellent. That evening, the whole camp got together for a quiz. Needless to say, our skills in general knowledge, were made to look extremely poor! The final morning was all about building a raft which had to cross a small stretch of river. Ours did survive the crossing but our result was affected by the huge amount of time constructing the beast. Departing the quaint riverside, disturbed by boisterous cadets, we arrived at the last activity, the van pull, where we had to tow a minivan over a set distance. Yeah, as a scrawny 14 year old I wasn't the strongest on the camp, say no more! With that complete, to conclude the camp exercises, we gathered for a small ceremony on the green before heading home.

Exhausted, I was glad to get home, but rather unexpectedly I felt upset to have left. The moral of my Air Cadet story, is that, even if you don't think that is for you, take a visit. I certainly wasn't the type to join, but I was so passionate to fly I joined. Most of the activities such as shooting were completely out of my comfort zone. But by leaving my comfort zone, I entered a challenging and exciting environment, something that's highly motivating and really builds your skills.

Although camps and all the other activities were fantastic, the real winner of my experiences with the cadets was the flying. I had three opportunities to fly with the cadets and I believe this was the time when I well and truly 'caught the bug' for flying. My nearest base for 'Air Experience flights' was RAF Wyton nearby to Peterborough. Upon arriving at the base, we had to pass a security checkpoint which cleared us over to the hangar, with a room for waiting and safety lessons. Once we are happy, and demonstrated our knowledge of safety we headed over to the aircraft with our flying suits donned, and met our instructor's for the flight. Luckily for me, on my first flight, I had a Virgin Atlantic captain, there was never a silent moment! After taxiing out and testing the engine, we powered up into the Cambridgeshire skies. This flight was special to me, as it was my first ever flight in a light aircraft. I was apprehensive to say the least. But I was truly blown away, as we skipped around the sky, viewing the world go by below. Taking control of an aircraft for the first time was a dream come true. The feeling of guiding a machine through the skies, which people look up to see, was a powerful feeling, giving me a hint of satisfaction. Being a military man, the instructor pulled an interesting landing manoeuvre. Arriving back on earth, I was buzzing from the exhilarating experience. I was ready for the next episode! For me, taking control of an aircraft for the first time added a new flavour to my taste of flying. It was no longer the feelings and views that were dominating my passion. It was the freedom in my hands, the satisfaction of control.

The Air Cadets was an integral part of the lead up to my current position as a private pilot. I suggest that anyone with a desire to fly joins the magnificent organisation, of which the government supports. Looking back, my biggest regret so far, was my decision to leave the cadets. Due to increasing work commitments, I was unable to say no and found myself struggling to maintain my work/life balance. I have now come to realise that there are many years to work, and that in your early years, you should focus on building your skills and having fun. I wish that I had stayed at the Air Cadets, because I would have developed more and more skills, and been exposed to more flying opportunities such as scholarships and Air Experience flights in more exciting aircraft such as the Sea King, and join the lucky buggers that get to join the aircraft during the Queens flypast! In terms of getting jobs, the air cadets can demonstrate to employers that you are keen, and have participated in many activities, highly desirable for them. Most notably, team building skills, uniform discipline and attention to detail. The Air Cadets is a recognised organisation and particularly an essential gateway into a career, I believe, for both military and civilian pilots. Crew resource management requires teamwork skills and cooperation with others, and the Air Cadets really help build these skills, making you a stronger team member.

Awards evening with the Leiston '1379 Squadron' Air Cadets.

Having left the Air Cadets around autumn, the winter went past and I cascaded into a world of work. As a waiter, I cherished my job, enjoying serving people and selling a great experience. This job has proved essential in my bid to become a pilot as a result of funding. Despite this, I was doing nothing for myself, just doing schoolwork all week, then working both days at the weekend. I thought long and hard for a few weeks and realised that I needed to fulfil my dreams, and act on them. Looking for ways to do this, I stumbled across the world of gliding on the Internet. Missing being up in the air, I was itching to get back in an aircraft and take to the skies. Although annoying my Mum in the process, each day before my birthday, I kept on asking and asking for a trail flight at the gliding club locally to me. Success! My mum finally agreed to it and booked a flight at my local(ish) club. However, weeks and weeks went past and every sodding Sunday the weather God had it in for me! Nearly 2 months passed until finally, the day come, the day when flying was taken to a new level for me. On an average, overcast, early spring day, I headed an hour and a half away to Rattlesden, where I had a trial gliding lesson booked. I was shocked to see such a basic setup! I had no idea that gliding clubs were so small. Following a tight country road, we managed to find our way to the end of a potholed, patched long runway, where a small white glider was parked, with a small yellow light aircraft sitting beside. But... Where was the clubhouse? There wasn't one! The clubhouse was the 1950s coach sitting up the edge of the old runway. Getting accustomed to the new flying environment, I went over to speak to the members huddled up in the coach, enjoying a cup of hot tea. "Hello you must be Ben" a welcoming lady said, with that, I introduced myself as I watched a glider bolt upwards on the winch. It was my first time witnessing a winch launch and parallel to some of the most exciting rollercoasters I've seen. With no engine, gliders are streamlined, fairly small aircraft made up of fibreglass. To compensate for the absence of an engine, gliders have super long wings relative to their size, this allows them to do exactly what they say on the tin. Glide! Compared to flying a normal aircraft, getting inside a glider is comparable to getting inside a tight canoe. A cramped space, cluttered with levers and pulleys, make getting in a challenge, but once in, it's quite comfortable, beings you are practically laying down. On a trial flight, the instructor will go through the relatively simple set of controls and instruments on a glider comprising of a control stick, rudder pedals, airbrake, trimmer, altimeter, airspeed indicator, compass and a variometer. With no engine, you may be thinking, how the heck does a glider get in the air then? Well, there are various options from being slingshotted off a hill to being towed by a car flooring it down the runway. However, the most common methods are, a winch launch and an aerotow. A winch launch includes a winch attached to a v8 engine. The engine pulls in a metal cable, connected to the glider, and as the wire pulls the glider it gains enough lift and gets to 1000 feet before the cable disconnects, this is certainly the most exhilarating launch method, being so fast and almost pointing into space like a rocket. The Aerotow is a little less intense, being towed into the sky, via a cable, by a light aircraft plodding along at 60 knots. The advantage is however, that on days with no or little thermals, you can get towed up higher or into thermals. On my trial flight I experienced an aerotow, which was lucky, because there was no lift at all! Getting towed up by the little yellow plane, we got higher and higher until the instructor pulled the cable, banked sharply left and levelled off, we were now gliding! The very first thing that strikes you when gliding is the peacefulness. Just the gentle flow of air gives a light whooshing sound, making its way around the canopy. Having a go with the controls I was surprised how agile and sensitive the glider was. The canopy gives fantastic visibility, which along with providing good looking out opportunity, allows those on experience flights to admire the scenery. The flight only lasted 18 minutes due the absence of lift. However, being back in the air, taking control of an aircraft was where I belong, and felt accomplished taking to the skies once more. But the real beauty of gliding was yet to be discovered. The cost! Once I became a member for just £60, my flights cost as little as £4! My longest flight 1 hour 12 minutes cost just £15 which in a powered aircraft would set you back over £150. It's obvious why this is, because you aren't paying for a fuel guzzling engine, spinning in front of you in a glider. You may be thinking, how in earth do you stay in the air for over an hour with no engine? Well it's back to those year six physics lessons. Convection currents. In the summer months the high, bright, strong sun heats up the ground, particularly the darker Matt surfaces. In turn, these heated surfaces, such as ploughed fields, roads and settlements, heat the air above them, causing the air to rise. Depending on the strength of the sun, this heating can be so strong, that the air rises at over

1000ft per minute. Inside the glider, we get used to the feeling of a thermal, turbulent and it's almost like going over a humped bridge. We also have an instrument, usually audible, called a variometer, to detect the amount of lift we are in. This lift takes the glider with it, meaning we get higher and higher and consequently can stay airborne for longer by flying around using various thermals. Although gliding is cheap, I think it is an essential part in my road to becoming a pilot. It firstly checked whether flying really was for me at a low price. All the lessons I have had, has built a plethora of flying skills that I select aspects from every time I fly. Gliding teaches you the importance of looking out for aircraft due to the absence of a radio. Gliding also makes you-work really hard to balance the aircraft using rudder control, to increase airborne efficiency. And I think most importantly, gliding forces you to make perfect judgements of height and distance, as you don't get a second chance at landing.

The leap of faith

I had many incredible experiences gliding, and I took a lot of skills on board. Some of the best flights were ones where we would circle the local area for hours in thermals. Gliding brings out the fun of flying in a different sense, due to the thermals representing a challenge to find, and use. One of my other favourite flying experiences was landing in a perpendicular crosswind, I will put a picture below to show my hand in line with the runway to demonstrate just how strong the wind really was. I built up nearly ten hours flying in a year. Around

Christmas time I discovered a great gliding scholarship, to get you to solo standards in the summer. This was part of the GAPAN scheme. But, there are many more funding opportunities, such as The Air League and Air Cadets. I spent evening after evening tirelessly perfecting my application, getting several industry experts to scrutinise my work. After a few weeks, I was happy and sent off my form. I anxiously waited as the weeks passed, to hear whether I had been successful or not. Around a month later I saw on my phone screen an email from the Honourable Company of Air Pilots, my heart was pounding and was sceptical to open the email to say the least. I read the email and felt disheartened. I had been unsuccessful in getting to the interview stage. Taking a moment to grieve over my lost opportunity, I tried to review where I had fallen short. Was my skill set too weak? Was my application poor? Or was it because, I had already obtained a generous bursary from my club? I however, quickly pulled my self together. I pondered over the thought of a quote I had read, stating that life is about not waiting for the storm to pass, but instead dancing in the rain. In order to dance in the rain, I had to move forward and make progress towards my prospective career as an airline pilot. With gliding so far away from where I live, and available funds from my hard work as a waiter, I realised that I could start my private pilot's licence. This would be the first step in my process of becoming a pilot, if I done the modular route, doing each licence step by step as opposed to an integrated course where you do every part of pilot training at once. I knew there was an airfield just 15 minutes up the road, and found a microlight school which is significantly cheaper than flying bigger aircraft like the Cessnas and Pipers. It was a fantastic start for me, with an incredible instructor, Gary, who has a real buzz and passion towards his flying. He was great to be around. After three lessons on the cheaper NPPL course, I realised microlight hours couldn't be counted towards a commercial pilots licence. Upset to leave Gary's great ambience, I stayed at Beccles airfield, but changed to the Private pilot's licence instead, where all my hours count commercially. To my delight, my new instructor was a Cessna Caravan pilot, working to my advantage several times, and had a wealth of commercial experience. We began by talking about my plans and headed out to the aircraft for a look around for any issues or problems. Once happy we took to the skies. I was treated to a spectacular view of the Red Arrows flying along the coast, although the Eastern Airways pilot at Norwich, that was told that he was number 13th to land, was probably not as chuffed. The first flights of the private pilot's licence are initially the most exciting before the first solo. Due to little experience, the instructors expect little from you, therefore you can almost take the back seat, embracing the views, having fun, flying a plane, possibly, for the first time.

When thinking about my decision to embark on my private pilot's licence, I often review the level of personal investment and commitment I have given and will continue to give. My friends and family are often shocked and amazed that I pay over £160 for each flying lesson. It often shocks me too! The common remark is 'you could be so rich if you didn't fly!' That is correct to a degree. Only if taking rich is a description of the amount of money I have. If take the word rich and look at its alternative meaning, I consider myself very rich indeed, where rich is the large amount of assets, (memories and experiences), one has and an asset being something valuable and useful to someone. The last few years my fellow aviation loving friends and I, decided to visit many places around Europe, using low air fares to absorb the whole experience of flight. On my own pin map, I added Manchester, Edinburgh, Athens, Heraklion, Bilbao, Barcelona, Corfu, Gothenburg, Marseille, Oslo, Turin, Grenoble, Madrid and Geneva. These 1, 2 or 3 day adventures were not a pointless, waste of money, but instead put me face to face with my hopeful future industry and have spurred me on with inspiration from the frontline. Having such memorable experiences are a huge asset, and I have no regrets in taking on such journeys whatsoever. As an aspiring pilot, I believe you have to assess the level of personal commitment you are willing to invest. Each person's situation is different. In my case, the private pilot's licence is a valuable stepping stone if I decide to follow the modular route, which may well be my only option. Therefore for me, the investment in a PPL, is very worthwhile.

Crosswind landing! See my hand in line with the runway.

Incredible sights over Cromer, Norfolk.

For a private pilot's licence, prices do vary, but as a rule of thumb the costs involved often mount to the £8000 range. For young people, this is a huge amount to raise, especially whilst still in education. So how did I pay you may ask? Work! I worked part time at weekends, and full time in the holidays, as a waiter in a busy seaside restaurant. Working is a good way to raise flying funds, because it motivates you whilst working and gives you a taste of the real world. It's good life experience and customer service roles work well, as often involves working with other people, which is an integral part of a pilot's day to day working life. However, balance must be achieved by ensuring work does not overrule your life and diminish any study commitments. Although I mentioned the Air Cadets previously, there are many other charities and organisations out there to support aspiring pilots funding their training. But there is a catch to this. There's major competition from people who have the same aspirations and dreams. Therefore it's imperative to stand out, by demonstrating your passion, dedication and ability to undertake such a task. Also mix in flavours of your personality and your achievements, if applying for anything, I can proudly mention the writing of this book, because there aren't many other 18 year olds that have written a book and had it published! Just be different, and catch the eye of the selection team! Scholarships are amazing opportunities that should not be missed, so you may as well apply to as many as possible.

From my experiences, I have begun to understand the way the world of aviation works. There are a small proportion of people who do not make the journey to become a pilot, whether that be for medical reasons, unavailable funding or lack of academic qualifications. But usually, the passion of aviation pushes these people into success in another field within the industry. Due to the high costs and stringent medical requirements needed to become a commercial pilot, I have considered my options and come up with a good contingency plan. I have a big interest in business, and so therefore, would love to pursue entrepreneurship, should becoming an airline pilot be unavailable to me. I did not initially consider this, however, I am very fortunate to have a very experienced mentor, from the real estate industry. Whilst busily working in the restaurant, James, my mentor, saw qualities in me, due to hard work. James, has given me invaluable advice and give me a perspective from someone who has a wealth of knowledge and experience in business, allowing me to develop key skills and competencies recruiters will be on the hunt for.

After the initial two or three flying lessons, something happened which really bugged me. I was treating my flying lessons as a burden. Each time I went to the club, I was spending £170, only getting home to see my savings, earned from over 2 years working, evaporate. Furthermore, having to work after some flying lessons made me feel rushed and uncomfortable during the lessons. So all those glorious images and feelings, described at the beginning of the book, where overrun, and my flying had hit a low point. It had to change, the greatest shame of all was the fact that it all came down to finance. This is when I discovered that all the financial and academic barriers to overcome to become a pilot are a good thing. They present a challenge, in which I am now having good fun, with a sense of achievement, to try and beat. No matter who talks about pilot training, funds always dominate the conversation. Young aspiring pilots like myself are left feeling frustrated and defeated by the £100'000 required funds that simply isn't available to them. I decided it had to stop though. Becoming a pilot shouldn't be a bubble of concern and doubt. Instead it should be an exciting challenge full of brilliant moments, where the young make the right decisions, and want to do something brilliant for their careers. Having an entrepreneurial personality, I decided I could use this to support both my pilot training funds and travel desires. My idea was an app. I am currently in the development stage of designing my app which allows people to request things in restaurants and hotels. By researching the app design industry and finding out the potential profit, I believe I'm onto a winner, you can see if it was a success in the next book in my series.

By this time, my flying had begun to move from the basics, as I moved into the circuit. On one particular cracking winter's afternoon, I turned up to the flying club to see the wind sock dead and deep blue skies above. Good weather is like a strong magnet that draws people to fly. Everything looks more beautiful when it's clear. I decided that it was far better to fly on these stunning, clear afternoons to get my money's worth and make it a more surreal experience. The best thing about them is that with many other people deciding to take to the air, the skies feel more alive, with club room chatter also a welcome difference from usual winter dead silence. Entering the clubhouse, I said my usual hellos and popped the kettle on before heading to the aircraft to carry out the aircraft inspection. There were several others carrying out the same tasks in the glorious sunshine. For the first time on this flight I decided to record the flight using my Go-pro. I did this for two reasons, firstly to look back on my flying for educational reasons and secondly to share my views and experiences from aloft. Due to delayed parachuting, my usual instructor, Stuart, arranged for me to fly with another instructor at the Club, John Wignall. On first appearance, John looked like he was ready for business. We went to the clubhouse to brief on circuits and shortly after walked out to our steed for the lesson, Cessna 150 G-AVZU. After the first 5 lessons, starting the engine and taxiing will all become independent, so I did just that! I started her up, taxied across the soft wet mud, did my engine run up tests and sat in the queue of six waiting for take-off! It was great to see each go sky bound, one by one. There are many exciting emotions when entering the circuit phase of training. Most notably, the first solo, that lay just hours away from achievement. But I think what dominates circuit training are the landings. Landing a plane has a thing about it which makes it a special moment of flight. Friends appear judge ones flying skills based on one's landing ability. Landing a plane is not as hard as many may think. Through intuition, although seemingly impossible at first, it becomes easier and easier to pull off a nice landing. Even seasoned veterans grin when they pull off an absolute greaser. Even though the objective is to get it down safely, it goes without saying soft landings always give any pilot a buzz. It's a challenge, and as with anything, smashing challenges makes anyone happy.

Having enjoyed the lesson with John, I returned home and filled in my logbook. Finally, I had finished my first page in my logbook, and had accumulated around ten hours powered flying time. My next few lessons with Stuart, covered the circuit, where I Practiced Engine failures after take-off, flapless landings, poor weather circuits and go-arounds. However, on the 8th of January, all this practice was required for something neither I, nor Stuart my instructor, could prepare for. Something potentially putting our lives at risk or at very least, the aircraft, the Cessna 172. Sat at the end of the runway, I pushed the throttle to full and within seconds eased back on the yoke to lift us up into the air. It was a routine take-off and all was normal. Stuart then pulled the throttle out and said, Engine Failure (a practice one). I pushed the nose down and desperately looked for a field to land in, Stuart added some flaps to help us get down in time. BANG! The aircraft rolled hard to the left, with a steep bank. Stuart immediately took control, added power and fought a little with the aircraft till he expertly used his commercial expertise to go through the aircraft security checks and recalled that when the flaps were selected when the drama begun. Stuart retracted the flaps and the aircraft returned to a normal flying state. I then took control, flying the aircraft downwind as normal, but instead, preparing for a flapless landing, which conveniently I had recently practiced. It was a perfect demonstration as to why we go through such training, always to expect the unexpected. I got the aircraft down safely in one piece. Upon inspection, the damage was evident, one of the cables connecting the flaps to the pulleys had snapped and was hanging freely, the flaps were essentially only held up by the airflow on one side. As you can see from the pictures, not the best flying state and could've turned out a lot worse. This situation was an experience for me that I took a lot from. It is human nature to always fail to accept that bad things may happen to us. It made me realise that whenever I fly, I should always brief on the ground and remind myself what I will do in certain situations, making me a better and safer pilot.

Not exactly what you want to happen to the flaps mid-flight!

Could I make it this time?

With bad weather over the following couple of weeks, I took the time to study for my communications exam and complete my application form for a PPL scholarship that I considered applying for. As aforementioned, I had applied to a gliding scholarship the year before and was unsuccessful at the first stage. This only fuelled my desire more though. I had done everything I could to demonstrate my passion. If spending £2000 of my own money on flying lessons, and starting to write this book at 16 doesn't show a massive desire to be a pilot, I said to myself "what does?" I had been lucky enough to meet a helpful man, James, who I mentioned before. We began to meet and discuss my future and his past, and make my future replicate his success and avoid his prior mistakes. My new mentor was instrumental in my ability to explain my situation to the selection panel in the best light possible. My passion and work ethic was undoubtedly present, but I needed somebody to guide me on how to present this in a few hundred words, not a 100 page book like this! After a few drafts and edits I had a sheet of paper that perfectly represented me and my situation. I wrote down all the things that I know would demonstrate my love for aviation, but at the same time, reasons why I needed to be awarded the scholarship, and why it would make such a big difference to my journey to become a pilot. I was both humble and honest. I didn't exaggerate, just simply believed in myself, and hoped that this won over the selection panel. I spent most nights for an entire month making tweaks to my form, before finally sending in my form at the last minute so that my form was fresh in the panel's minds, if they read them upon receiving them of course. After a few days, I was happy to receive an email from the Honourable Company of Air Pilots saying that my application had been received and that I would be notified as to whether I had been successful or not in around a months' time. The anxious wait began. And things started disastrously. I received a call. It made me feel distraught. It was from my flying instructor at Beccles, who you may remember, Stuart. He began by saying he was sorry. And that he had bad news. Beccles airfield hadn't been able to sort its paperwork and therefore was shut for training purposes, and only open for those hiring or using their own aircraft. My local airfield now wasn't an option. I would have to travel miles to fly. It wasn't a nice situation. Stuart however, shared the news that he was joining BMI and got a job on the Embraer E145, so I was pleased for him after waiting over 10 years to get into the commercial world of flying, having built an incredible wealth of experience in bush flying, parachuting an instructing. I said my farewell to Stuart, then spend the next week extensively researching local flying schools, if you count an hour away as local! I opted to shortlist Earls Colne in Essex and Norwich in Norfolk as my two preferred choices.

However, now I was almost 100% reliant on the fact that I would win a scholarship to make my continuation of training possible, due to added travel costs, as well as the greater expenses from flying out of a commercial airfield. I had around a week to go till I heard back from the scholarship selection board and was feeling anxious. Not ideal when I should've been 100% focused on my revision for my AS-Levels, but I learnt to deal with it and put my head down, studying hard up until the day where I was told that I would hear back. It was the Easter holidays and I was off work, revising most days. The day I would expect to hear back came. I checked. No email. Next day, I checked and no email. The day after that I check and no email. The weekend passed. Monday came, no email. Then on a Tuesday morning whilst working hard on maths work at my desk, I heard a notification sound on my computer. I didn't bother looking though. After about 10 minutes, I went to unlock my phone to look at my Facebook adverts. There on the screen in bold. 'Honourable Company of Air Pilots'. The email had arrived. The email that would determine the next year of my future. In the short preview, I read the words thanking me for the application. My heart began to race, had I fallen short at the first hurdle again? It was one of the more intense moments of my life as I slowly stepped towards my computer, anxiously anticipating such news that could either make me feel on top of the world or give me a sinking, broken feeling. I saw the words congratulations, I walked away, laid on my bed, and tried to calm myself down. I was ECSTATIC! I didn't even read the email properly before racing down the stairs to let my stepdad know the news. He was just as excited, and was almost as surprised as me for such good news. I ran upstairs and read the email fully, my heart skipped a beat, I was off to London in a months' time for an interview. What an experience it would be. Furthermore, if I could win the scholarship, it would change my life!

It was around a month before my interview. Life was getting busy for me. I had to study for my AS levels, work on my business and now prepare for the interview. I however, put my studies first and used the few hours I was awake before school to write bullet point after bullet point about things I should mention to the selection panel. I also spent time watching hundreds of videos on YouTube about interview techniques, and how to answer difficult questions. I was very fortunate that my mentor and an ex Royal Air force fighter pilot very kindly offered to simulate an interview for me at their homes. This proved to be valuable experience before the big day. It allowed me to deal with questions I couldn't prepare for, and practice on the spot thinking to deliver the very best answers. During the debrief with my mentors, they kindly advised me to keep the answers honest, short and to the point and if possible, show off my personality through the answers in which would be desirable as a pilot. Despite all the preparation for the interviews, I still didn't feel ready. Reading the past winners stories, their experiences made me even hungrier for this chance of a lifetime to gain a PPL over the summer, and I didn't want to fall short at the final hurdle. On the night before, I got excited for the rare opportunity to go to London in a suit, in first class on an intercity train, entering a very posh building to sit an interview which would enable me to live my childhood dream, becoming a pilot. How cool is that! Having woken up at the crack of dawn, to reach London via a three hour train journey, I made sure I dressed to impress. I chose my best suit, put on my polished shoes and headed for the train station. I felt part of the business community upon arrival, mixing in with the businessmen on their daily commutes to the Inner-city. Once on the Inter City train, I had a table to work from, whilst I reviewed my notes I had made on how to portray myself in this interview. I discovered, the interview is an opportunity to impress the panel in a record short time. Therefore, self-confidence is paramount. If you are proud of your achievements, no matter how big or small they may be, the way you tell the story will be far more convincing and commendable, rather than if you doubt yourself and end up waffling. I felt this would work for me, being a passionate person anyway. It was my time to shine.

Whilst I cannot disclose the aptitude test and interview contents, I can give a brief overview of my experience and what you can expect. Having enjoyed a Wetherspoons breakfast, I made my way to Cobham House, the home of Air Pilots, nearby to the Chancery Lane tube station. The building itself is nestled amongst other important looking buildings, with thick doors and decorated brickwork. Upon entrance, you have time to sign a few items of paperwork and chat to a few of the other candidates. You then sit a short aptitude test or interview first depending on the order of candidates. The aptitude test consists of items usually covered in other pilot written aptitude tests and wasn't overly difficult. The interviews take place in Cobham house's grand rooms, wonderfully decorated, full of character. You then return to the reception, collect your things, and leave. I was lucky enough to meet another young man called Stan, who I chatted with, whilst we waited for the other candidates to arrive. We left the building together and filled each other with confidence, whilst we walked through the streets of London like investment bankers, in our sharply ironed suits and briefcases hanging by our sides. We then bid farewell and headed our separate ways. It was an experience that I will never forget, and was thankful even to reach that stage, and have the opportunity to go for an interview in such a remarkable building. Naturally after an interview, you begin to doubt yourself. On the train journey home, I started to contemplate whether I had delivered the right answers and had done enough preparation to answer the questions. I distracted myself, by doing some revision for my upcoming geography exams. I was anticipating the response taking around a week. However, I couldn't stop thinking about it. I had to watch YouTube videos and read blogs to find ways to deal with the anxiety that kicks in after an interview. After a day or two, having had several conversations with Stan and my friends, I started to calm myself. Instead of doubting yourself and thinking of the situation in the worst case, think of the positives. Don't dwell on the negatives. The previous year when I was unsuccessful at the application phase, I didn't give up, instead, I thought immediately about the next year's application, and how I could make it better and make my application stand out better, over the previous year's one. I started using all my wages for PPL flying lessons to show my passion and dedication to the industry. I started writing a book about my journey in becoming an airline pilot, to inspire other aspiring pilots, and in turn, show my care and interest in other people's journeys. I started my own business to show my ability to think outside the box, in order to pay for my flying. I would bounce back even better and even stronger for the following year and boy did I do that! Can you see now the effects of making a positive out of a negative situation which has the potential to make you upset, disappointed and maybe even lead you to give up on potentially, massive, opportunities? Don't do it. Bounce back better!

Several days after the interview these thoughts entered my head, if I was unsuccessful, I would devote my summer to working, investing in my business, eventually being able to fund my own training, albeit over a longer period of time than the scholarship would allow.

It was around four days after the interview and I had a geography lesson, where we were revising for the upcoming exams. As we were packing up, I spoke to my teacher about his business that he was setting up. I decided to show him some tips and tricks online, to help him with his website, using my phone. I had an email notification. I was really excited because it was a sale notification from my online store. I had made $10 online. That felt awesome! After finishing my conversation with the teacher, I walked back to put my things away before heading home. I opened up my email app to see what the order was for and I WAS SHOCKED! I had received an email from the Air Pilots as well. I quickly opened it, read it in a flash and my heart skipped a beat! I had been awarded a scholarship for a PPL, to complete, over the summer of 2017! It meant the world to me. I immediately shared the news with Mr Webster and my friend Harry who happened to still be in the room. I was in such a flap, I left my keys in the classroom before I drove home. I didn't really trust myself to drive anyway, whilst I was still shaking with excitement. It was a dream come true and instantly became one of the best moments of my life. I turned up the tunes and took it steady, whilst feeling on top of the world. When I arrived home, I reluctantly told my step-father as if the good news had to come out in a more formal moment. Instead, I decided just to tell him as I walked in. He was equally as happy, congratulating me on the matter. My mum received the news in a slightly less civilised fashion. She found out via Facebook. Yeah. You can imagine what she said as she burst into my room. "I had to find out on bloody Facebook didn't I?" I just said "power of social media ay, your fault, went on Facebook as you walked in, rather than seeing your son." All I can say is you win some, you lose some. I certainly won earlier that day, but lost this. Gents, women are always right. Ok. Got that? Perfect!

After a few days the good news had sunk in; I was ready for the incredibly exciting, but busy, summer ahead. There was one thing in the way though... AS Exams! I had already obtained my Class 2 medical, so was all ready to start the flying. With a month to go until my AS exams though, my attention had to sway towards preparing for them once more. Using pilots Instagram's to inspire me that if I worked hard for my exams, I would end up like them, and Simon Mayo's drive time show to lift the boring silence, or in my case, block the incessant whining of my little sister, I studied every single night for 2/3 hours straight. Failing to mention the six coffees a day and pack of biscuits. Soon enough, the exams finally came around and as quickly as they came, they were over. Reflecting on them, I had been confident in geography and physics but found the maths papers especially difficult. It wasn't my happiest time. I felt disheartened and disappointed that I couldn't have achieved better. I felt like I had messed up my grades, and left a bit of a sour taste in my mouth for a few days. But then I decided to do what I done last time, take a positive out of it. Why was I doing a maths A-Level? You don't need it to be an airline pilot. As a pilot, calculations and measurements are an integral part of the job. So I decided, not being a maths genius, if I took a Maths A-Level, it would improve my number skills and mental maths ability, making my training and future job much easier. Taking this into consideration, I had worked my socks off in preparation for the exam, learning a great deal, becoming much better with numbers. I had been successful. A simple letter grade was far less important than skills, that would help me for life, I gathered. I had smashed my goals. I won. It didn't matter to me anymore which grade I got, because I knew deep down, the very reason why I decided to take that subject; and I had fulfilled what I wanted out of it.

Anyway, enough of that talk, just before my final exam, on a beautiful summer's day, made even more beautiful by the fact it was my first Saturday off work since what felt like the stone age, I took a trip with Nigel, the ex RAF fighter pilot from my village, to go and look at two potential flying schools, where I'd spend the summer learning to fly. After the typical hardship of bobbling along single tracks full of potholes to find an airfield, always seemingly difficult to reach, nestled away in the middle of nowhere, we reached the first airfield of the day, Crowfield.

Crowfield is around an hour away from my home, situated on a farm. It comprises of two grass runways, something I wasn't initially keen on, and has a welcoming, surprisingly modern clubhouse. Having taken note of where the tea and coffee was, yes, I had my priorities straight, me, Nigel and the airfield owner Andrew, walked out to the hanger to take a closer look at the aircraft that the airfield operate. THEY HAD GPS! Instead of the worn, cramped, mossy cockpit of the aircraft I had previously flown, the Robin HR200 at Crowfield was modern, built in the last 20 years, that's brand new compared to the 1967 aircraft I was used to, had plenty of mod cons including a GPS and had a clean polished paintwork. I was impressed. If anyone needs an airfield salesman, I recommend the Williamsons of Crowfield Airfield. They sold the airfield to me extremely well, putting to bed my doubts about the grass runway and the fact that the airfield only has one instructor. The next airfield to look at, Earls Colne, was 40 minutes up the road from Crowfield. Whilst cruising up the road Nigel and I discussed the pros and cons of Crowfield. I can tell you, the entry road to Earls Colne is certainly a pro. Instead of splashing through muddy puddles, rocking around the road from all the bumps, Earls Colne's entrance has a security checkpoint, brand new tarmacked road, with a grand hotel and spa, along with an 18 hole golf course. How Posh. Upon pulling up at the Earls Colne Airfield clubhouse, I was surprised to see how busy it was. It was a hive of activity. Engines purring, rotors chopping, phones ringing, briefings discussed. With over ten instructors and aircraft, Earls Colne was the busiest general aviation airfield I had experienced. Finding some quiet, tucked away in an office, I met the chief flying instructor and discussed my position. We concluded that Crowfield was better option, due to being closer to my home, however, Earls Colne was definitely my reserve. It was impressive to see such a slick operation. Reflecting on the day, it soon become apparent that Crowfield airport would suit my needs better, due to it being closer and smaller. What excited me most about the day, was the prospect of me spending around five days a week, at the airfield, in the gorgeous summer sunshine, whilst working hard to work towards my PPL.

Having completed my final AS Level exam soon after, I was faced with a decision. My manager asked me what I was available over the summer. In my mind, I felt I could've dedicated the entire summer to flying and got away with not working. However, I felt if I was to keep my job, I could save up money to fly after I got my PPL. So said I'll do 30-40 hours a week. Equating to around three days a week. Allowing me to fly for the other four days in the week.

I had around a month left of college and opted to start flying twice a week. One Saturday and one Thursday, where I had a permission to not attend college. What was incredibly helpful, was that Crowfield offered me the chance to book double slots on my flying days. This meant that I could accumulate hours more quickly, allowing me to reach the required 45 hours before the October deadline. My first lesson at Crowfield took place on the 15th of June.

The best summer of my life

Saturday the 15th of June. The first day of my flying scholarship 2017. Feeling excited was an understatement! I woke up early after a late night working hard on my business, and dressed smartly to go to my job as a waiter for breakfast. Of course, I got rather distracted by customers, as when the conversation was focused on me, they were incredibly interested in my flying aspirations. Having served a restaurant full to the brim of cheery holidaymakers, I headed home at noon, cycling through the village, in the gorgeous sunshine. 32 degrees it was. Hotter than Tenerife or Marbella! I arrived home to a lovely BBQ. Once I wolfed down a few burgers, burning myself in the process, I headed to my room to grab my supplies and briefed myself on the hour-long car journey. Three times the length of my furthest drive. Exciting and nerve-wracking! After filling up the curse jar during the journey due to a complete lack of competence by some weekend drivers, I finally arrived at Crowfield Airfield, near Stowmarket, for my 3pm flying lesson. I had booked an hour-long lesson, and got started straight away. I met John, the instructor, and we had a quick chat about myself, my experience and my aspirations. John is the Chief flying instructor at Crowfield. Because the airfield is fairly quiet, John is the only instructor. This is a good thing, because throughout my training John knew exactly what stage I was at, and what my strength and weaknesses were. This makes training a lot more efficient as far less time is spent recapping. I was slightly worried however, because if John was to fall ill, my training would come to a sudden halt. Despite this, I had plenty of confidence all would go well, with John very athletic and energised. John was not short of experience. His career started flying in East Anglia on turboprops for local companies such as Air UK. He then went on to fly Boeing 737s for major European carriers such as Fly Globespan and Ryanair. All very exciting for me, with a dream to follow in his footsteps and become a commercial pilot. Once we learned a little about each other, we headed out to the aircraft for the day, the Robin HR200, G-MFLE. John gave me a quick tour of the aircraft so that I was familiar with the controls and instruments. The engine start and taxi was familiar, once I got into it, and after backtracking the runway we entered the greenhouse after closing the canopy! It was boiling! Anyway, it didn't bother me at the time, as we were about to head sky bound, and after applying full power, it was a few seconds before I entered my second home again after five months. It was my most enjoyable hour in the last five months. The flight consisted of climbing and descending, turning, stalling, slow flight, engine failures after take-off and circuits. Yes, it was as busy as it sounds! But John made it great fun. The control stick in the Robin was comfortable to use, and the thing that particularly stood out about the aircraft was the incredible visibility from the cockpit. Once I showed John what I could do from my previous training, we headed back to Crowfield, landed, and parked up next to the fuel pump to fill her up for the next day. Upon landing, John made it clear that I was approaching solo level and that I should work on the three exams I was required to pass in order to fly solo, so that I can conduct my first solo in the next few weeks, following my first flight at Crowfield. This was exciting news and was great start to my summer of flying.

15.6.17 my first experience flying a Robin HR200.

However, despite a good start back in the air, there was a blockade to my progress. My dreams of flying solo in the coming weeks were halted. The requirements of the Air Pilots stated I needed to pass three exams (Human Performance, Communications and Operational Procedures) before I could fly Solo, in order to balance theory and practical skills. How was I going to pass three exams in a few weeks, when the others had previously taken a month to gain adequate confidence in the same situation? Working smart was the answer. Using apps and textbooks, I spent two hours for each exam gaining the concrete knowledge. The essentials. The things that would come up over and over again. Once I had this base, I could slowly introduce the smaller, less talked about concepts. And to my surprise, it worked a treat! After a few weeks I passed the first 2 exams at 100% and 96%.

Armed with 15 hours in my logbook, the required exams and full of enthusiasm, the first solo was looming. The best experience of my life (at the time) all started on the 5th of July, a nice day, though with plenty of cumulus clouds popping up as the temperature began to rise. Driving to the airfield, I was feeling unusually tense. Not only was I potentially going to fly on my own for the first time, but that luxury was subject to my ability to pass the final theory exam, which I felt somewhat ill prepared for, given my short period to prepare for it. With a nice strong coffee, I looked at my notes on operational procedures, and pondered over my knowledge to pass the exam. Failing one of the easiest theoretical exams would be pretty embarrassing right? Furthermore, having to write a progress email to the Air Pilots, telling them I hadn't flown solo due to failing an exam was not something I particularly wanted to do. I decided, sod it, I can do it! In a small, poorly lit, cupboard like exam room, I scribbled down my name on the exam paper and opened it up. I resorted to counting up those I was 100% on to see if I could pass or not. I felt anxious as I opened the door and handed over the exam to John. After checking the mark scheme, he said "well done, 100% on that one." Although happy to get full marks, I felt more relieved to know I could now fly solo and sustain my progress.

With the boring stuff out of the way, it was time to get airborne. The plan was to complete some circuits and see how I got on. In my mind the objective was to impress John enough to let me fly solo. However, in the back of my mind, I resisted this somewhat. John offered me some comfort. An experienced pilot, overseeing my actions. If anything went wrong John would come to the rescue. Just like Stuart had with the flap failure at Beccles. However, if you want be a pilot, you have to make your own decisions and react to any abnormalities. I convinced myself that John wouldn't put me in danger by allowing me to fly solo with inadequate experience and skills. We proceeded to complete some practice engine failure after take-offs, normal circuits, flapless circuits and glide approaches. After one final good normal approach, John asked me to taxi to the parking area before he said "Do you want to do one on your own?" Although I was expecting this, it still caught me by surprise. It didn't feel real. Was a 17 year old lad really being allowed to take a tonne of metal in to the sky, on his own? Despite being apprehensive, I agreed that I was ready. After exchanging some words of advice, John said "You'll be fine mate," before opening the canopy and hopping out the back of the aircraft. What followed was the weirdest feeling I've ever felt in my life. I was sitting in an aeroplane, on my own, with the engine purring, about to take-off. Just looking beside me to see the seat empty, felt completely alien. Once I had a minute to get use to the new experience, I prepared the aircraft for take-off, setting the flaps, checking the mixture was rich and the carb heat was off. With the air traffic control fully aware that a first solo was about to hit the skies, I gave them a quick call to say I was about to depart. Once acknowledged with "G-MFLE, roger, report airborne" I responded with "wilco (will comply)" before checking I hadn't missed anything, again and again. Having slowly got accustomed to being alone in the cockpit, I was now sat at the end of the runway, looking down the grass strip, poised with the task of safely completing a circuit. Taking a few seconds to compose myself, I decided it was time. I pushed the throttle to full, and within seconds, I was hurtling down the grass strip. Finally the big moment came, I eased back on the control stick, disconnecting with earth and becoming airborne. Like a rocket, I shot up to 1000ft rapidly, due to the reduction in weight without John (no offence). Once I levelled off, I had a minute to evaluate the situation. My lifelong dream was to become a pilot and there I was, in a plane, acting as pilot in command. A little smirk followed as I pondered over this fact. Then on the downwind leg, I refocused, made my radio call and completed the necessary checks. I had taken off ok, managed to get to the downwind position without incident but was now faced with the next and most challenging part. The landing. Descending towards the runway, I set the flaps, slowed down and lined up for my final approach. My position and height was perfect. I felt relieved, now all I had to do was land and park up. After a faultless flight, seconds before touchdown I had to make a big decision. Land or Go Around? Not used to the lighter aircraft, as I flared the aircraft, I began to gobble up runway as the aircraft floated centimetres above it. The runway was getting smaller and smaller. Could I make it? Seconds before applying full power and making another attempt, the wheels made contact with the runway. With a sigh of relief, I gently applied the brakes before vacating the runway. After alerting the Air Traffic Controller I was safely on the ground, I received congratulations. "G-LE thank you and well done." I saw John marshalling me towards the fuel pumps. I followed his instructions before coming to a halt, completing the checks and switching off the engine. I had done it! I had safely completed my first solo. I was buzzing! John hopped onto the wing, before opening the canopy, to give me a handshake and "Well done young man" he said. I decided to point out my floating antics that he probably noticed. "You were just a few centimetres off the deck" John replied, as he demonstrated with his hands. The first thing I done after speaking to John, was to rip the Go-Pro off its mount, and confirm it had in fact recorded this memorable life event. At that moment, I knew my training had really taken a turn now. It was time for the real flying. Navigation. Finally, rather than being stuck in the circuit, it was finally time to fly further afield, see new scenery, land at different airports and even mix in with bigger commercial traffic. It was all very exciting! There was certainly no time to celebrate, because after a nice chat over a cuppa, it was time to get airborne again, this time to prepare me for the coming months and teach me how to navigate. The flight was good fun, and every time I matched the place on the ground with the place on the map, it felt incredible. Although, it was funny getting ones wrong to which John replied in one instance "Bloody Diss, that's not even in this county."

Pre-flight checks before departing on a solo flight to Norwich.

The next month, and ten hours flight time, was spent building solo experience and getting used to navigating. In order to gain a Private Pilot Licence, you are required to have a minimum of ten hours solo flight time. Commonly, student pilots enter a solo consolidation phase shortly after their first solo, to build both experience and confidence. In my case, this consisted of circuits, designed to practice landings and small local navigation exercises. Leaving the circuit, for the first time, by yourself is a unique experience. It's a bit like driving to school alone for the first time. It's familiar territory, but you're alone, trying not to make any mistakes. Once I began to grease my landings (make them less hard), John set me the challenge of flying a navigation exercise covering nearly 80 miles, taking just under 1 hour. This was my first flight away from anywhere where I had flown before. I had to make radio calls to a radar control I was unfamiliar with, use a map to navigate from points on the ground I've never heard of before, let alone seen, all whilst flying safely and efficiently. Monitoring speed, heading and altitude. The flight went well. I managed not to get lost, and all my timings and distances worked out. However, the thing that caught me by surprise most, was being able to find the airfield at the end. It's just a grass field amongst other grass fields! Slowly, panic started to set in. I was 'LOST'. I desperately scanned the area back and forth, using a few reference points John had pointed out to me. Just as things started to deteriorate, losing altitude without noticing, whilst frantically looking for the small grass strip, my eyes locked on to it. I didn't have to call Wattisham air traffic control and request a heading back to the airfield. My pride was saved. At least that's what I thought at the time.

Now, I apologise to any pilots reading this because you would've heard this many times. There is no such thing as pride in decision making as a pilot. You should never consider 'your pride' as part of the decision making process. Whether it be other pilots listening to you on the radio as you're lost. Corporate passengers not reaching their destinations. Being stuck away from base. It doesn't matter. Make the safest decision. As pilots, it's our responsibility to operate in an efficient way. But when conditions prevent us, or forces us, to do something in order to stay safe, respect it. Looking back at my incident of being momentarily lost, I should've acted much quicker, rather than getting panicked. Hypothetically, I would've been able to hold more pride in requesting a heading back to base, because I would've been operating more safely, and not putting my personal pride first. This flight illustrated, that although the focus was to develop my navigation skills, I learnt a lesson about pride. It shouldn't exist in aviation...

It was now August, I had 25 hours of the required 45 in order to gain my licence and life was good. I has having the summer of my life, flying almost five days a week. It really was a dream come true. Something I was really looking forward to in my training, was flying to another airfield, stopping for a bit, before making the return. The 2nd of August was my first opportunity to do this. John and I flew to Old Buckenham Aerodrome, a small, but busy airfield in the south of Norfolk, twenty minutes away from Crowfield. The purpose of visiting other airfields during my training, was to make me familiar with the various different procedures at new airfields, for both once I had gained my licence and as part of training for my cross country qualifier assessment. Despite grey skies and gusty winds, we braved the conditions to safely arrive at Old Buckenham. Having arrived at Old Buckenham, the true power of flight hit me. A fifty minute road journey had taken us just twenty by air. There I was standing next to an aircraft I had just flown in challenging conditions, to arrive somewhere completely different from where I was twenty minutes before. The whole A to B excitement exists because of my aspirations to become an airline pilot. One of the qualities of the job, that I love so much, is the prospect of being somewhere utterly different in a matter of hours. Whether that be leaving the grey oppressive clouds of Luton for the turquoise seas of Santorini or Snowy Scotland for Arid Arabia, the transition of time, season, culture, and atmosphere excites me. In no other job, can you wake up in the morning, have a coffee in your lounge, before taking off, landing somewhere 30 degrees warmer, with a contrasting culture, before making your way home, and enjoying a coffee before bed in the same lounge you left in the morning. I cannot wait for the moment to be sitting in that lounge, looking back on my days flying and my first land away gave me a taster of the notion of moving from place to place via the air.

Having made my first land away, the next ten days were intensive, leading me to acquire just under ten hours flight time and visit three new airfields, including Great Oakley, Peterborough Connington and Norwich International. New challenges popped up, having to navigate airspace, receive directions from air traffic control and land on tricky runways. The contrast couldn't've been starker, between the rugged grass runway, set amongst the farmer's fields, at Great Oakley, and the long, clean cut asphalt runway at Norwich. Furthermore, hopping out of the aircraft in Norwich, results in VIP treatment. Leaving the apron and striding into a small terminal, made for passengers using private jets, is a real treat. Free luxury food and drink, what more could you ask for? Meanwhile at Great Oakley, after squelching through the boggy grass to the reach the small shed like building, you'll get as much as a cuppa tea. Both airports offer something different though. Their own challenges, luxuries and views. I really then was starting to see the sheer beauty of making landings into new airports.

Having navigated the skies of Suffolk, Norfolk, Essex and Cambridgeshire to struggle to locate, often hard to find, grass strips, John told me I was ready to complete my cross country qualifier flight. As part of training for the private pilot license, pilots are required to make a solo flight to two different aerodromes, before returning back to base, with the total round trip having a total distance of more than 150 nautical miles. In order to satisfy these requirements, my proposed route took me initially seventy miles away to Peterborough, stopping for a refreshment, then continuing onwards to Norwich, raiding the minibar, then making the final leg back to Crowfield.

The 29th of August. One of the hottest days of the summer, with the mercury hitting a delightful 30 degrees. Some would say it was perfect conditions for my cross country qualifier flight, but I beg to differ, after sitting, in essentially a mini greenhouse, for over two and a half hours, bathing in my own sweat. #PilotProblems. I rose early, eagerly checking the weather, in anticipation of my most exciting flight to date. I saw the temperatures were high, already 20 degrees at 7am, and apart from few low cumulus clouds, the winds were light and the skies largely clear. Armed with a nice cup of coffee, I carried out all the preparation I could, including reading the airfield charts, checking the airspace notices and the expected weather. All the planning, and the fact I was making two full stop landings, made the situation feel closer to the commercial job I dream of.

Arriving at the airfield, I met Neill, the airfield operations manager, and John, who both fuelled me full of confidence by giving their recollections of their cross country antics. John called both airfields to warn them of a juvenile pilot on the loose, wishing to land on their runways. The aircraft for the day, G-MFLA, was in tip top condition and ready for a long day of flying. However, this particular aircraft didn't have a GPS, so reaching the destination was solely dependent on my map reading skills. The first leg was estimated to take 45 minutes and warranted a straight out departure. At 10:45am, I, inside G-MFLA, leaped into the clear Suffolk sky, bound for

Peterborough. First things first, I announced that I was airborne to Wattisham approach. Wattisham air traffic control were providing me with a basic service. A basic service is where you check in with controllers, who then update you on weather and airspace information, usually also giving you details on conflicting traffic, despite it still remaining a pilots responsibility to prevent collision. Climbing up to two and a half thousand feet, I levelled off, confirming my position with my map. Luckily, the first town to fly over was Bury St Edmunds, a large town with very distinctive features, including one of Britain's biggest sugar beet factories. So far so good. The theme of nice distinct features continued. Ten minutes later, I passed over the world famous Newmarket racecourses, whilst chatting to the American controllers on the Lakenheath Radar frequency. In a reassuring, professional, American accent, the controller released me from the frequency. "Gulf Leemah Alpha, You're are leaving my airspace, free to change frequency, squawk 7000." A squawk is a code that we input to the transponder to allow air traffic controllers to identify us, with a unique identity. 7000 is the basic code for light aircraft flights in the UK, although controllers often give new codes, to specifically identify us. Having changed over to Cambridge air traffic control, I was now north abeam the city of Cambridge, half an hour into my flight, bobbling along at 2400ft at 100 knots. The flight was going well, however, I was now faced with a potential problem. The remaining thirty miles of the flight was over a very sparse landscape. Known as the fens, the area south of the Wash, spreading south into Lincolnshire, Cambridgeshire and Huntingdonshire, is characterised by its flat, repetitive, agricultural land. It was twenty miles before reaching the next major town, Huntingdon. With no major visual cues, I was flying almost blind, relying solely on my pre-flight calculations, which are often not one hundred percent accurate. Luckily, close to Huntingdon, two former air force bases exist, RAF Wyton and RAF Alconbury. Soon enough, I confirmed my position, using the two airfields to identify

Huntingdon in the middle. Having been cruising for the past half hour, things were about to get interesting. I was now turning overheard RAF Alconbury, speaking to the radio operator at Peterborough Connington, preparing for my arrival. Using the A1M motorway below, I carefully navigated towards the airfield, now lying just miles ahead. Connington accommodates a flying school and club, a helicopter school and an aerobatics school. This coupled with its geographical position, acting as a confluence of air traffic, makes the airfield and the surrounding airspace notoriously busy, especially on a hot summer's day, which it was! I now had to balance safely flying the aircraft, whilst completing my approach checks, whilst trying avoiding other traffic. By listening to the radio, I managed to paint a picture of the traffic situation in my head. There was an aircraft ahead of me descending into the circuit and one a fair way behind me, with several others already in the circuit. The procedure at Peterborough, requires traffic to fly overhead the start of the runway, before turning around, descending to fly perpendicular over the runway, half way along it, before joining the circuit half way along. Luckily for me, the same runway that John and I used on the previous visit, was active. Subsequently, I was familiar with the procedure, having done it before. "G-LA descending dead side" I announced to the radio operator as I started my descent into the circuit. Becoming anxious of conflicting with other circuit traffic, my head scanned back and forth to double check the radio calls matched up with the aircrafts true positions. Confident I could slip into the circuit, I made my way to fly downwind, flying parallel, in the opposite direction, to the runway. Landing checks complete, traffic calls made, the last few turns turned, the runway now laid straight ahead of me. Briefly distracted by an intercity train hurtling along the East Coast Mainline below, I regained concentration, carrying out a smooth, stable approach, before gently touching down on Connington's long, bumpy, concrete runway. "G-LA, Welcome to Connington, continue taxi to vacate and hold Charlie."

Essentially, an old runway crosses the active runway at the end. I was instructed to turn off onto the old runway, make a 180 turn, before holding short of the active runway, waiting for an aircraft to do a touch and go, then taxi back up the runway toward the parking area. Next, came the hardest part of being a private pilot. Parking! I asked myself, "Where the bloody hell do I park?" Thankfully, a friendly soul was on the other end of the radio waves, and kindly obliged to offer me continuous taxiing instructions to reach the correct area. Fifty minutes after the engine sprung to life in Crowfield, I cut the mixture (fuel) to the engine, and let G-LA have a quick nap. It was an immensely satisfying feeling having just navigated sixty nautical miles, using just a map, to safely arrive into Peterborough. In my hopeful mind, set on becoming an airline pilot, I was now on the turnaround, giving myself a Ryanair slot of 25 minutes. Having pushed the aircraft back in line with the others, I secured the aircraft, and grabbed the stuff I needed, before walking over to the clubhouse, where I would pay the landing fee and get my form signed.

When undertaking the cross country qualifying flight, an official document needs to be filled in by the air traffic controllers at each airfield, to confirm that you behaved yourself.

With the radio operator at Peterborough satisfied with my flying, the landing fee paid, and a cold beverage consumed, ten minutes of the turnaround remained, so it was time to give the aircraft a quick once over before waking her up for the next, 40 minute leg, across to Norwich. I hadn't ever flown between Peterborough and Norwich, let alone the surrounding airspace. Therefore, I was apprehensive about the flight. I was, however, uber-excited to fly over new places, seeing more of Britain from above. Things didn't get off to a good start… After 3 start-up attempts, the battery slowly discharging and a growing audience wondering what was happening, fear started to set in as I couldn't get the engine to start. Had I missed something? Was the engine broken? Was I going to have to ask for help? I waited a minute, whilst conjuring a plan to go and ask for help in the clubhouse, should the next attempt fail. After an anxious couple of minutes, I turned the key. The same whining sound followed, however just before I gave up, the propeller came alive, and with a couple of coughs, the engine sprung into life. "Thank god for that" I sighed, as I began my checks. Giving way to the Grob Tutor passing in front, I hesitantly began my taxi to carry out my power checks at the holding point for the runway, worried I was going to get in the way of any aircraft wishing to vacate the runway. Happy that all the indications were as they should be, it was time to head skywards once more. Lining up behind a landing Extra 300 aerobatic aircraft doing circuits, I waited a few minutes to avoid any risk of collision, before applying full power, getting airborne within seconds. With everything a little more congested around Peterborough, making the flying become even more of a juggling act, climbing up to 2400ft clear of Connington, allowed me to relax somewhat. Despite having never flown in the airspace, the route was rich with features and the airspace itself was quiet, let alone the great air traffic control service from the nearby RAF Marham. The route initially took me across the desolate fenlands to Wisbeach, then Kings Lynn, before cutting across to Norwich, routing beside the Queens residence of Sandringham. Similarly to the previous leg, the light cumulus cloud was growing in thickness, and forced me to fly a little lower than my planned altitude. Although fun dipping above and below the small clouds, it gets incredibly bumpy, as you may've experienced in airliner, when flying in the clouds. I opted for the smooth ride to Norwich, and dropped a few hundred feet, below the clouds. After a relaxing, enjoyable thirty minutes of uneventful flying, cruising above the fens, I grew closer to Norwich, where things started to get more involved. After absorbing the magnificent views of Sandringham from above, I became slightly unsure of my position. Great Massigham, West Raynham or Foulsham, which Airfield was below me? My calculations made Great Massingham seem the obvious choice, but the features below didn't match up! Uncertain for a minute, I was able to pinpoint my position using the large town of Fakenham. But the challenges didn't stop there. I was now faced with another problem. I was racing towards Norwich's Airspace at 120mph, but didn't have clearance to enter. I had no option but to enter what's known as a holding pattern. Using the village below, Foulsham, which sits on the edge of Norwich Airport's airspace, as a marker, I began flying around in a circle, whilst waiting for permission to enter the control zone. Because Norwich is a busier airport with Helicopter, Charter and Scheduled operations, it has a layer of protection in the air, which is controlled by highly trained air traffic controllers to keep air traffic separated. My turns were getting less and less tight, as I begun to get slightly dizzy, completing a good ten tight circles in the air! With an apology for the wait by air traffic control, they cleared me to enter the controlled airspace, fly directly towards the airfield, and report when I could see it. Even from 2000ft with decent visibility you can see in excess of thirty miles, so I had no difficulty finding Norwich Airport which spans 280 hectares. Reporting that I was visual with the field, I was cleared to fly the right hand circuit pattern and report when on final approach with the runway. Everything felt fairly familiar, when flying the circuit, doing the checks and making the decent towards the runway. Then, as I lined up with the runway, it hit me! There on the taxiway, a Flybe Embraer E195 jet, with over 110 people on-board, waiting to jet off to Alicante in Spain, was waiting for me to land on the 1800m long asphalt runway (three times the length of Crowfield's grass runway). Knowing that some excited passengers were probably peeking out the Flybe, watching me fly the approach, I felt that I had to nail the landing! Gently easing the throttle back, I raised the nose to let the aircraft float centimetres above the runway before kissing the surface. It was a greaser! Knowing that some holidaymakers who would rather be in Alicante than Norwich, were sitting on the runway behind me, I taxied with some sense of urgency, before leaving the runway at the end and making my way to Saxonair, the handling agent for light aircraft at Norwich. Being marshalled into my parking position between a Bombardier Cl604 business jet and a Metroliner Turboprop airliner was quite an experience, requiring precision to avoid any hiccups between the five million pounds worth of aircraft.

Norwich remains to be one of my favourite places to fly to. The reason? Well, you feel like a true pilot! After shutting down the aircraft, I was escorted by one of the friendly Saxonair operations staff to the private jet terminal. Yes, you heard that right, as light aircraft pilots you get to use the private jet terminal! Free drink and light snacks, beautiful, upmarket décor with stunning views across the airfield, it's a real gem of a destination. After helping myself to a nice ice coffee, I made my way to the reception to pay the £20 landing fee, and ring up the air traffic control to book a departure slot, something you have to do in a controlled airfield such as Norwich. Filling my pockets with some gorgeous buttery Scottish biscuits, myself and Jon, the operations supervisor, headed outside to get the aircraft ready for the final leg of the day, back to Crowfield. Before this, Jon took me over to the Challenger business jet to have a look around. Typical. I had forgot my bloody phone to take pictures of the sparkling jet. It was stunning to get up close and personal none the less. Despite getting access to many aircraft in hangars, such as Lufthansa and Titan Airways, the excitement still remains when I get to have a nosey around an active commercial airliner. As the day was getting better and better, it was also drawing to a close and after bidding farewell to my new pal, it was time to get ready to fly back home. Giving the aircraft a quick once over, starting up and receiving taxi clearance I made my way to hold short of Runway 27. Completing my checks, soon enough I was cleared to takeoff and lifted off for the third time that day.

Giving way to a helicopter that had also just departed Norwich, I made my turn out over the city of Norwich, directed towards Crowfield. Having left the relatively busy Norwich airspace, using the A140 road as a ground feature, and reaching cruising level, it all became rather leisurely. I was familiar with the area, controllers and all the ground features. It felt just like home! The entire flight was akin to this, safely arriving into Crowfield just twenty minutes later.

It felt good to be home. Feeling accomplished, having just navigated 160 miles across the East of England, I popped inside the clubhouse to receive a warm welcome from John and Neill, congratulating me on making it back in one piece. John proceeded to check my form and brought a kind comment, from the Norwich controllers, to my attention. They left a note on my form acknowledging my level of competence. This was warming to hear as the next challenge was dawning on me. The test! Luckily I had to build a further 10 hours of flight time, in order to have the required 45 hours to take the test, giving me the opportunity to sharpen up my skills. I booked a few lessons for the following week, and headed home for a well-needed ham, egg and chips!

A Flybe Embraer E175 at Norwich Airport, viewed from the Saxonair apron, taken before the final leg of my QXC.

It was good having John back with me. Having spent the last five hours alone in the cockpit, it was nice to have somebody to speak to, as well as to critique certain aspects of my flying, in order to improve upon them. My steep turns were a bit sloppy and my radio navigation was getting a bit rusty. Spending the morning tightening up on these skills, which would be assessed in the skills test, in true aviator fashion, John and I retired to the clubhouse to enjoy a coffee and our new favourite doughnuts, which I had discovered in my local service station. As the conversation moved onto cars, almost coincidently, a loud sounding car entered the car park. Naturally, all swinging around to see what it was, John remarked "Ah that's Mike, got his new flashy car." Exiting his Mercedes AMG, Mike entered. "Afternoon all, I'm flying to Duxford today, but I have nobody coming with me, anyone know who would like to come along?" He proceeded to explain how he planned to fly with his son, but being a lazy teenager, he was still in bed gone midday. I wanted to jump up at the opportunity, but had booked an afternoon lesson booked with John, two hours later. However, probably as a result of my enthusiastic body language towards the prospect of flying to one of aviation's most famous airfields, John turned to Mike and said "Why don't you take Ben? He has got a lesson later, but we can delay it a little." I slowly nodded to demonstrate my interest without coming across over keen.

Twenty minutes later I was sitting beside Mike, Climbing out of Crowfield bound for Duxford. I was super excited to be flying to Duxford. Having visited several times in the past, I was looking forward to once again 'being the over side of the fence'. Having avoided a busy gliding site, we took a direct track towards Duxford and were on approach in no time. Just 25 minutes after leaving Crowfield, we were now on a straight in, long final approach for Duxford's Runway 24 left. Testament to its tourist attraction, The Imperial War Museum at Duxford has been able to invest in high quality, modern infrastructure consisting of an impressive, long asphalt runway, linked perfectly by several taxiways. The taxiways themselves provided one of the highlights of the trip. Having dipped down, just metres above the M11 motorway, Mike gently touched down and taxied to the end to vacate the runway. Being the summer holidays, with suitably 'summery weather', (no, not rain, sun), the museum grounds were full of families enjoying a day out. Several of them were lined up along the fence watching the aircraft take-off and land. Whilst taxiing to the parking position, I had the pleasure, as well as Mike, to wave back to the children and their parents. What's so special about that, you may be thinking? For me, it was all about looking back and seeing my former self. I was obsessed with planes, and still am. After watching planes all day at Duxford, I would rush back home to jump on my simulator and try and re-enact what I had seen, and now I was doing it for real! With my level of progression of my prospective career in front of my very eyes, it was a very special moment for me.

There wasn't time to cherish the moment for too long, because, in the distance, a violent storm was rolling in. Large cumulonimbus (storm) clouds were building up on the horizon, and we had to escape Duxford before they reached us. We had an estimated half an hour, to pay our landing fee, prepare the aircraft and depart Duxford before the storms arrived. Although a little disappointed we didn't have time to enjoy the museum at Duxford, I was still on cloud nine about the impromptu visit. As soon as we had arrived, it was time to head back. After taking pictures, posing with the 'only pilots allowed signs', we hopped in the aircraft and started the engine. Having completed the checks, we lined up with the runway, pointing directly towards the incoming storm. Luckily, we were heading home in the opposite direction, so after reaching 1000 feet, we turned around back towards Suffolk. I did feel like a poor antelope trying to escape a lion, as the storms chased us back to Crowfield. Dodging a few localised showers on the way back, we got home without incident, despite being thrown about by the choppy, turbulent air. Guzzling a quick glass of water, it was my time to take to the controls. We had to be quick. The storms that chased us back to Crowfield were edging more and more east. John and I decided it would be best to complete a short flight around the local area to practice skills that would be assessed in the skills test. For the next hour we tracked radio beacons, flew on instruments in the cloud and buzzed farmhouses, as we swooped low overhead, during practice forced landings. It had been a full days flying, with nearly 3 hours airborne. What a day! However, there was no time to sit and rest, my radio exam was rapidly approaching, the penultimate test before I was issued my licence.

Arriving into Duxford by plane for the first time. Note that I am the other side of 'the fence'.

In order to gain a Private Pilot's Licence, it's required that you complete a practical test, in order to get a flight radio telephone operator licence. Luckily, Crowfield has a resident examiner, Irwin Jones, so I didn't have to travel far to conduct the test. Irwin is a British Airways Airbus A380 captain, who visits Crowfield around once a month to do communications revision and exams. Communications is a vital part of aviation, to ensure flight is both safe and legal. There are many different procedures, and so phraseology to match. I spent countless evenings prior to the exam poring over example routes, with various situations happening along them. Complementing this with 15 minutes of YouTube before bed each night, I felt ready for the Sunday morning exam.

It was an early start. We planned to start at 9am on the Sunday morning. However, I arrived 45 minutes early to get prepared for the occasion. Driving carefully through the early morning mist, every situation possible passed through my head, as I rehearsed my lines one by one. Another student, Paul, was also completing the test. Having arrived and equipped myself with a coffee, I sat with Paul where we discussed each of our concerns and problems that we were having. Whilst filling each other with confidence, Irwin made a warm welcome. "Good morning chaps, I'll grab a drink and come and sit with you." Having grabbed his essential morning beverage, Irwin sat down and explained the process, before asking if we had any problems that needed fixing. After clearing a few slight misunderstandings with Irwin, he handed Paul and I the route that we would be 'flying' and for the record, no, we didn't do any real flying. I sat in one classroom, as a pretend pilot, flying a pretend route, whilst Irwin, sat in another room, as a pretend controller, linked up to each other by some high tech radio communication equipment.

Once I had ten minutes to get to grips with the route and note down any necessary useful pointers, it was time to put my radio skills to the test. Apart from being naturally nervous, it did take me a few minutes to get over the fact of sitting in a room, with a mic sat in front of me, like some sort of criminal giving my police interview. Once familiar with the equipment, the test begun. It honestly couldn't've started any more disastrously. I had requested engine start, but completely skipped the radio check, which Irwin began to explain is a legal requirement. Praying Irwin had given me the benefit of the doubt, and apart from missing the MAYDAY MAYDAY MAYDAY part off my emergency call, I continued to complete the test without any mishaps. Until, in some weird Indian accent, Irwin crackled across the radio "G-BD go around, I say again, go around sheep on the runway." Luckily, the sheepdog rounded them up during my go around, and the test was complete upon landing. I took off my headset and went for a debrief, with Irwin, in the other room. Although wanting to confront him about his Welsh accent, which in fact resembled that of a nation the other side of the world, I decided to avoid doing myself any injustice in hoping to pass. Despite a few blunders along the way, the cliché handshake proved I had passed. Paul also then went on to pass his test.

I decided to question Irwin on his welsh accent, "You scared me Irwin, I thought you were taking the mick about my inability to communicate my navigation and I ended up in New Delhi," he laughed as he signed the relevant forms. "Well done chaps, you now have your radio operator licences." I was ready. I had everything I needed to gain my PPL except a few hours of flying experience.

Now, despite having around five more lessons before my skills test, consisting of a mixture of solo and dual flights, one flight in particular stood out. It was my final solo flight before my skills test. After finishing college I drove straight to the airport to get my final hour in. Although warm and sunny, this induced a few localised showers, so the flight required some shower dodging! Once airborne, I headed straight for the coast. The sea looked unusually blue as I flew above it. What become apparent throughout the flight, was how relaxing it became. Rather than trying really hard to manage my speed, heading, altitude and checks, everything flowed naturally. Subsequently, I was able to enjoy the views far more than normal. The showers sprinkling the unlucky towns below, the lorries overtaking other lorries, with a tail of cars winding behind, the various operations taking place at the Felixstowe port, all visible as I looked down from above. With hours of superb instructing from John over the summer, I was glad that everything had come together, and enabled me to fly with a lot of confidence. This was needed as my skills test was booked for two weeks later.

It was no good. As I sat laid on my bed the night before my skills test, I felt terrible. I had posted in a Facebook group asking a few questions about the skills test. I received several blunt responses, telling me I should know the answers, and shouldn't be conducting the skills test at all. It was getting later and later, the winds were gusting 30 knots outside and I was not in a happy place. Luckily, checking my phone before bed, several others had commented on my post, telling me to ignore the so called 'Sky Gods' ignorant responses, and instead, praised me for reaching out to admit my insecurities. Although somewhat comforting, I was still nervous about the gusty conditions. After eventually managing to drift away into a snooze, I woke up to the same whistling wind. I decided the conditions were inadequate for the test to take place, so I called the examiner John, yes another John, and rebooked the test for the following Monday. Although the conditions were marginal, I decided that the winds would make the flight even more hard work than it needed to be, not to mention at times it exceeded the wind limits for the aircraft. At least I had a week longer to prepare myself.

With the next week whizzing past since the cancellation of my previous test, the big day had finally arrived. The weather was clear, with light winds, the route was planned and most importantly I was fairly confident, helped by the calm conditions, and no, you're not the first to think I'm a fair weather pilot. It's just... Easier! After giving John a ring, I set off to the airfield. We planned to meet at 8:30am for the test to commence at 9am. Setting off early to grab a sausage roll from my favourite local garage, I arrived at the airfield 50 minutes later - a few minutes early. I met Ian, the part time airfield operations manager, who was busy preparing the aircraft and clubhouse for the influx of activity due later in the morning. Kindly, Ian had prepared, fuelled and checked over the aircraft for me, prior to my arrival. As I busied myself checking over the performance charts for the Robin HR200, I heard John pull up in the car park. Just like my driving test a few months prior, it all became real as the examiner turned up. Conveniently, I had met John several times before when I was gliding and this, coupled with his laid back personality, helped ease my nerves. Although, they weren't distilled completely, as I still had a huge amount of pressure heaped on me. The Scholarship sponsors, my family, my friends, the staff at Crowfield were all waiting to hear my fate in the coming few hours.

Once John was happy with my take on the weather, route and performance calculations, we sat down at the clubhouse table for the briefing. For the first part of the test, I would fly a standard departure initially routing to Cambridge, where overhead the airfield I would turn towards Old Buckenham. Around half way along this leg, John said he would tell me to divert to a random point, requiring me to plan this appropriately. Once happy with the diversion, John went on to explain how he would then examine my general handling skills including: steep turns, slow flight, instrument flying, practice forced landings and practice engine failures after takeoff. And if that wasn't enough, I then had to complete three circuits consisting of a glide, flapless and finally a normal landing. Wow. I thought my driving test was hard….

Although I knew I wasn't going to fail the test for it, I had made a bit of a fool of myself when John asked, "What if you can't fly above the minimum safe altitude?" I replied, "Turn back and come home." He laughed "If everyone did that, nobody would ever go flying!" Managing to forget my blonde moment, we headed outside to complete the exterior checks. Although it was nothing more than circling the aircraft, reading off a checklist, being followed like a duckling by John, around the aircraft, did make me feel slightly uneasy. Every now and again he asked me a simple question about the airframe, which I managed to deal with, until one extraneous question about the ailerons, to which eventually John admitted "I don't know either."

Happy with the condition of the aircraft, it was time to hop in. However, it wasn't that simple. John was playing the role of a passenger that hadn't flown before. As a result, I had to brief him on the flight, in terms of safety as well as comfort, not to mention he could play the pure ignorance game. Luckily, John reflected a good passenger, one that did as he was told and didn't question anything, which meant, getting seated was straightforward. One thing I enjoyed most about solo flying was that I didn't have to worry about the instructor getting bored whilst I snail paced through the checklists. With John by my side, I was glad to see he was waiting patiently, whilst fiddling with something trying to keep occupied. Once everything was ready, it was time to start the engine. I shouted "clear prop," placed my hand on the throttle and twisted the key. Nothing. Just an electrical whine that almost demonstrated my inability to start an aircraft. Great start. Fortunately, cold aircrafts sometimes require some patience to get them started, and this time I got it on take two. With the taxi and power checks going smoothly, I contacted Wattisham Approach for a basic service, ready for the trip towards Cambridge. "G-LE, MATZ penetration approved and a basic service, report airborne." I had my second pair of eyes and was cleared to enter military airspace.

As we bounced along the uneven grassy runway, I turned to John and asked "You ready?" He was happy to go, so after swivelling round at the end of the strip, I elected for a rolling, immediate departure. Hopefully for the final time as a student pilot, I pushed the throttle to full before lifting off into the cold sky above, where my fate would lie in the next 2 hours. I climbed to an adequate height, before turning back overhead the airfield, so that all my route calculations were accurate from the starting point. Cambridge was situated 35 miles to the west and with a strong headwind was due to take 32 minutes. Not forgetting anything in the climb, things got off to a good start and soon enough I was able to relax somewhat as I levelled off at the cruise altitude of 2400ft. The navigation to Cambridge went as well as it could've done, as we arrived directly overhead without any 'lost' moments. I gathered it must've been ok as John began playing with the pitot heat switch, watching it mess with the compass alignment, presumably to keep himself occupied. Upon reaching Cambridge, I made my turn to the next point, Old Buckenham airfield. The stress began to mount at this point, the next leg was much more featureless and I had a matter of minutes to gain clearance to enter Lakenheath's military airspace. Whilst wiggling around Newmarket, trying to work out the correct heading, I'd never been so glad to hear an American ladies voice. Usually it was my American lady boss, Lynn, asking me to work. Sorry, Lynn. This time, it was the controller giving me clearance to enter military airspace towards Old Buckenham. Approaching a nice feature, the ex Honington air base, John told me to divert to Bentwaters, an ex-Cold War base for the US Air Force. Making the quick calculation, I needed to take an easterly heading for 25 minutes. Looking at John, he remained expressionless, neither proving nor disproving my hypothesis. It soon become apparent that I was way off track, probably ending up 20 odd miles away from Bentwaters. Applying a 10 degree correction half way along, I managed to salvage the diversion and ended up reasonably accurately overhead Bentwaters, albeit, over ten minutes early! Oh well, I made it, I thought to myself, reassuring myself that John would have some leeway.

John looked over and said "Good, you'll get there ok. Right, I've got the radio now, just concentrate on the flying." To begin with, I completed a few simple turns, climbs and descents, before climbing up to 3500ft to do some stalling recovery, one with power, and one without. Miraculously, I managed to remember the pre stalling checklist, which I had forgot every single time I flew with instructor John. Having dropped like a brick a few times above the Suffolk countryside, it was time to don the 'foggles', fogged out glasses for the non-pilots reading, and fly using just the instruments. Simulating flying into cloud, John told me to do a 180 degree turn, using just the instruments to escape the potentially dangerous situation. Proving to be no problem, I then had to navigate using radio beacons, taking me towards Stansted, once more proving to be not a problem. There was just one main thing left to do before heading back to the circuit, the beloved practice forced landing!

At three thousand feet, nearby the birthplace of coppertop (Ed Sheeran), Framlingham, John pulled out the throttle and said "Right, your engine has gone." Getting the aircraft stabilised and gliding along at seventy knots, I started to look around for suitable fields to go into. Luckily a nice long patch of grass presented itself as the perfect opportunity. Having completed the pretend mayday call and engine restart drills, the ground was growing closer and closer by the second, as the tonne of metal I was sitting in, was gliding along surprisingly well, so well in fact, I was too high to land! Having made a series of S turns and deploying all the available flaps, I was still too high. I decided that I had to whip out a specialist technique known as 'side slipping'. Effectively, it involves using the rudder and ailerons in unison to skid through the air, reducing speed, allowing for a quicker rate of descent. Using this technique, I managed to dip very low, above a field before John instructed me to climb away. Retracting the flaps, I got the aircraft into a steady climb heading back towards Crowfield. Suddenly the power shut off. It was John again! He shouted "Engine Failure," doing the correct procedure, John was satisfied I could deal with an engine failure after take-off, which was being imitated, and we really did then finally head back to Crowfield.

I had been flying for over two hours, and the nature of the test made it both mentally and physically exhausting. I kept my chin up though as I approached Crowfield, with just three circuits left to complete before the test was over. Having read a frightening story of a private pilot failing part of his test, for joining the circuit incorrectly at the end, I was getting increasingly anxious as I approached the circuit. There are many different ways to join the circuit, however, John asked me to join via the overhead. Although confident with the procedure, I was unsure what to do. Due to my position, lined up with the same direction with the runway, I could just descend on the dead side downwind, something I explained in the cross country chapter. I turned to John to ask him, simply to receive shrugged shoulders and a blank face, "you're the captain, you make the decisions." Not wanting to repeat the story I read up, I elected to carry out the full lengthy procedure of flying the entire overhead join circuit pattern. That way, I could be confident there would be no question over safety. Soon enough, I had descended to circuit height, crossed the runway and was downwind. John had told me to make it a normal landing to begin with, a good start to ease me in. Being a quiet airfield, Crowfield's circuit was vacant of any other aircraft making the workload easy to manage, keeping my focus solely on to aircraft operation. Announcing that I was downwind, I completed my checks and made my final descent and approach to runway

31. Following a nice, precise landing, John retracted the flaps, whilst I applied full power, climbing out for the next circuit. Once level, John requested a glide approach. This meant, that whilst flying the circuit and confident I could glide to make the landing, John would remove the power, and I would glide back to make the landing. It didn't go well at all! Having told John I was ready, I stabilised the aircraft, turning perpendicular with the runway. Replicating my earlier PFL, I was way too high, forcing me to chuck down the flaps and side slip my way in. Somehow, I got the aircraft down successfully, and took to the air for the final time. "Make this a flapless one," John asked. Essentially it was to practice in the event of flaps failure, meaning the approach would be more flat, to keep the speed under control. Announcing that I would be making a full stop landing to Wattisham Air Traffic control, I proceeded to make a decent flapless landing and expedited my taxi to the parking area. Had I passed? In fact, having been in the aircraft two and a half hours I was more desperate about the fact to have a wee. I was bursting!

I did have a moment of confusion shortly after. John being a very laid back, calm man, congratulated me and said well done, but never actually explicitly told me whether I had passed or not. Having switched off the aircraft, collected my stuff and quickly nipping to the loo, I met John back at the reception, where he was filling out some forms. Ian looked up at me "Congratulations Ben, well done." That's when it all sank in. I had definitely passed! I could not believe it, I was now a real pilot, a dream from my childhood, a status I admired from behind many airport fences and now I had joined the club! I was ecstatic. I spoke with John and Ian about the licence application before making way, back to college, an hour's drive. Unlike passing a driving test and having to be driven home by your instructor, you can drive after passing your skills test whilst literally on cloud 9, requiring some level of discipline to stay focused! After forty seven hours of flying, ten exams, stressful situations and the gift of a scholarship, I had finally done it. It was perfect timing that I had a holiday to Majorca in two weeks, time to relax!

Despite not setting foot in an aircraft for over a month, whilst I waited for my licence to be processed, the following few weeks were incredible. I had many conversations with my family, friends and locals about my training adventures. An increasingly common theme was peoples shock when they realised that I could fly an aircraft on my own at the tender age of 17! My usual response was "You'd rather see my flying than my driving!"

A selection of photos from my first few experiences as a private pilot. Taking Friends and family for some flights over Suffolk.

Now, I could go on to tell the stories of my first few flights as a private pilot, but that's in my next book, which has already been started, taking you through my journey, hopefully from a private pilot, to a fully qualified commercial pilot. Instead, I think receiving my PPL is a nice finale to the book, and I rather take the last few pages to summarise the key learning points I took away from my experiences.

Listed below, are my personal 5 top tips which I would give to any aspiring pilot.

1. Ignore the rubbish.

    The human mind isn't very good at filtering crap. Unfortunately, when people act like they know what they are talking about, we tend to automatically trust them. Unless of course you are super sharp. And you have to be! Throughout my training, countless people have tried to put me off with silly stories that just reflects their lack of dedication. Guys. Look at the facts, become sharper at spotting crap! It can seriously send you into a world of disbelief for no reason whatsoever!

2. The earlier the better.

    Don't hold back, don't be lazy, start early, the more you can do, the younger you are, the better impression you can make. Naturally, people's expectations of teenagers is very little. Messy rooms, lie ins and drunken parties. This prejudice is a blessing. Why? Because it means whatever you do that shows focus, passion and drive, makes you shine above the rest. The older you get, the harder this becomes, as the baseline raises. So get a job, start buying a few flying lessons and start a blog!

3. The journey is the fun

    This one might just be me, but here's a little food for thought. Everyone has made a cake at least once. Why? More than likely, it's a nice thing to share with your parents or grandparents on a quiet Sunday. Cake is lovely, but isn't rubbing in the butter with your fingers, whisking in the eggs, with mixture flicking everywhere, licking the spoon halfway through, the fun part? Course it is! Flying is no different. I envy anyone undergoing flight training right now, that was the super exciting time, as this book has shown. Don't rush it. Embrace it.

4. Network

    The scholarship I won, was mentioned to me by a friend in my village. The person that helped me win that scholarship, I met in the pub. The person that helped me write this book, I met, again, down the pub. You get the picture right? The more people you meet, the more opportunities that present themselves.

5. Document

    By simply keeping a diary, noting down why I made the decisions I made, and why I felt the way I felt, I've been able to make changes to improve my chances of success. For example, I decided to start my PPL after not getting the gliding scholarship, because I wanted to progress, instead of sulking. By writing this down, I know that for every failure, I can work the same magic and turn as many negatives into a positive. Furthermore, documenting your journey makes you think more about what you are doing, again forcing better decisions.

To those who have helped me

There is no doubt, that without the generous support of all those that have helped me, in my pursuit of becoming a pilot, I wouldn't have made it. Although, some may feel they played a small part, I am eternally grateful and would like to pay tribute to them in these final few pages.

If somebody told my younger self that I would become a private pilot at 17, I would've laughed in their face. Despite working hard to earn money to fly, ever since I was 12 years old, shovelling horse poo down the local stables, the level of finance required for a PPL is almost unattainable for young people. The Honourable Company of Air Pilots (HCAP) made the seemingly impossible a reality. Although it's easy to look at their support as a free PPL, to get me started, it's far more than that. The scholarship has enabled me to get started on a journey I would've otherwise struggled to get started on, and has given me the hunger to pursue the rest of my training. I would like to thank the Honourable Company of Air Pilots for the opportunity, from Angie who worked extremely hard to organise my summer, to those who fundraised to finance my scholarship, I am forever in debt to you.

Vision. That's what my incredibly supportive family have. Although not being able to support me financially, every single family member was there, at a flash, to help me out. Whether it was my Mum, giving up her Sundays, to take me gliding, my uncle taking me plane spotting, my Grandad and Grandma taking me to Duxford, or my Step Dad driving me back and forth to Air Cadets, everyone had faith, that their dedication to support me, would be worth it in the end. Although it's sometimes hard for me to show just how much I appreciate it, you are all true diamonds, and I owe a lot to you all.

Throughout the duration of my scholarship, I was faced with several challenges, which I needed to overcome, in order to progress with the flying. Luckily, a duo from my incredibly supportive community, reached out to help me. Firstly, my mentor James, played an instrumental part in the application phase. He was there to read it through, highlight the positives and sieve out the negatives. Furthermore, he was always willing to give up his time to help me develop new skills, sponsoring me on courses, driving me hours away to complete them. Nigel, a highly decorated ex fighter pilot, also stepped in. Similarly, Nigel sponsored me on courses, held mock interviews for me, along with his wife, Margreet, and helped me find a suitable flying school. A very kind gesture, all very much appreciated. Jan Etherington, a highly experienced writer, also played a role, making sure this book was readable, offering her support as an editor. Thank you people of Walberswick, I couldn't dream of a more supportive community!

Having always wanted to fly, it's only right to thank those who taught me. Whether it be Gary and Stuart at Beccles, coping with my woeful attempts at landing or John at Crowfield, sitting beside me for over 30 hours, constantly reminding me of little nuances, the instructors that taught me to fly done a fantastic job of keeping me safe, motivated and enthused. I would like to extend my thanks to Andrew, Ross and Neill at Crowfield for helping me complete the scholarship at the airfield they manage.

As with all lists showing gratitude, I have probably unintentionally forgot somebody. But as long as people know I appreciate their support, I'm happy.

Thanks for reading everyone! Hopefully, the next edition won't be too far in the future…

Printed in Great Britain
by Amazon